Now is the Time to Practice

Dharma Reflections inspired
by Định Quang Temple

Text Only Edition

Also from the anniversary series of Định Quang Temple:

Awakening the Lotus:
Mindfulness verses inspired
by Định Quang Buddhist Temple
(ISBN: 979-8842224166)

Abiding in the Dharma Treasure:
A Self-Guided Tour of Định Quang Buddhist Temple
(ISBN: 979-8848599534)

Now is the Time to Practice:
Dharma Reflections inspired by Định Quang Temple
(ISBN: 979-8333213372)

Now is the Time to Practice

Dharma Reflections Inspired by Định Quang Temple

David Ketchum (Thích Giác Viên)

Springfield, MO, USA
ISBN: 978-1-967588-01-5
Welcoming Path Press

Nam Mô A Di Đà Phật

In gratitude for
the gift of the Dharma,

we respectfully bow
to all who have supported
ĐỊNH QUANG
BUDDHIST TEMPLE.

We are especially
grateful to our teacher,
VEN. TỲ KHEO
THÍCH THÔNG CHÁNH.

Returning to and relying on the
BUDDHA, DHARMA, AND SANGHA,
we aspire to practice deeply
for the well-being of all.

Contents

PART 3: CELEBRATIONS

PART 4: GRATITUDE & SHARING MERIT

Foreword

Namo Sakyamuni Buddha

Practicing the Buddha's way, we gradually remove the entanglements of the ego, starting from the coarse to the subtle, from the nominal to the real. The coarse and the nominal are things that can be seen and heard from the body and mouth. The subtle and real are abstractions of the mind, of consciousness. Practicing transforms our body, speech, and mind from evil to beauty and goodness; from greed to generosity and goodwill; from anger to compassion and patience; and from ignorance to joy, equanimity, and wisdom. Practicing is a process of change: from cause to effect, from the ordinary to the holy, from ignorance to wisdom, and from false attachment to liberation. To practice is to break down the nominal and gradually peel off the ego, letting go of illusions and false names. If undertaken to compete for fame and power, even great actions do not reach the goal of practicing for transformation.

Cultivation is meaningful when each action, word, and thought is consistent with the Dharma, aiming for the benefit and happiness of all beings. But if they are not based on the Bodhi mind, actions are just delusions born of ignorance and attachment. Reflecting on how change happens in the world, we can examine our own ideals and aspirations. In the storm of impermanence arising all around us, happening right before our eyes, what should we do, say, and think to sustain our practice and be worthy of these fragile moments of life? Knowing the importance of spiritual friendship in the Buddha's path, we have written a few things for everyone to learn and practice together.

This book is the result of much support from the Venerable Monastics and Buddhists of the Vietnamese and American communities. We sincerely hope to receive further guidance from monastics and good friends: to help us on our path of learning the Buddha's teachings, to be more diligent, and to shine the light of Buddhism everywhere.

Venerable Thích Thông Chánh
Abbot of Định Quang Buddhist Temple
October 2024

Acknowledgements

With a deep bow, I offer boundless gratitude and respect to the Buddha, Dharma, and Sangha.

To the Most Venerables and all the monastics of the Midwest Sangha, especially to my Thầy at Định Quang Buddhist Temple, I am deeply grateful for your extraordinary wisdom, compassion, generosity, and patience as my practice and understanding of the Dharma deepens.

To all the members and friends of Định Quang Buddhist Temple, I am grateful for the unspeakably wonderful gift of a place to practice, and a community with whom to practice.

To the English-speaking community at Định Quang Temple, I am grateful for your encouragement and feedback as I offered these reflections as part of our weekly Dharma class.

To numberless teachers and translators, and especially those listed in the Notes, I am grateful for your generous and skillful effort that make these teachings available and accessible.

To Max Prater, I am grateful for your work designing the original format for the anniversary book series.

To all who read and practice with this book, I am grateful for our mutual interest in and commitment to cultivating wisdom and compassion, on the bodhisattva path that brings complete freedom from greed, hatred, and delusion.

To all who offered feedback, corrections, and editing expertise, I am grateful for your patience, insight, and corrections. Thank you also for ongoing corrections for any mistakes, incomplete understandings, and confusing expressions that remain in the book due to my own limitations.

May all beings, in every place and time, practice in such a way that brings about a complete end of suffering.

Introduction

The mindfulness verses that form the basis of these reflections were composed in 2022 and featured in ***Awakening the Lotus***. To write each verse, I would spend time in meditation, using the subject of the accompanying photo as an object of awareness. This practice gave me an even deeper sense of gratitude for the profound gift that Định Quang Temple offers to the Ozarks.

When I first visited Định Quang for Ullambana in 2011, I knew only a little of the rich depths of practice held in the images, ornaments, and offerings that filled the halls. I had studied Buddhism academically during graduate school in the late 1990s; I started practicing with the Buddha's teachings in 2005, largely in the context of socially engaged Buddhism; I then lived in Cambodia from 2007-2010, immersed in a Theravadan culture and practice. I was a stranger to many of the Buddhas and Bodhisattvas, Dharma instruments, altars, offerings, and practices that now surrounded me. Despite this ignorance, Thầy generously invited and included us into the temple community, and, drop by drop, the bucket started to fill.

In 2017, Thầy invited a small group of us to open an ecumenical, English-speaking service at the temple. This brought with it the rare and wonderful opportunity to learn from and practice closely with him and, over time, other monastics of the Midwest Sangha. I cannot adequately express how grateful I am for this, and I can only hope that the fruits of their generosity are expressed in my practice and glimpsed in these reflections.

Each chapter of this book contains a mindfulness verse, related reflection, and then questions (to support contemplation) and practices (to support application). The reflections are offered through the lens of my own understanding and practice; they are not definitive, but invitational. Our goal in publishing this book is to give to others a starting place for deepening their own practice, especially those unfamiliar with Vietnamese Buddhism, with the encouragement that they will do so with the support and guidance of a temple and teacher.

We also encourage you to adapt the reflective questions and practices to your needs. If only one question resonates with you, that is the question to contemplate. It is better to do one practice wholeheartedly than all the practices superficially. And for those able to do so, the book can also be used in a group setting. Most importantly, the reflections, questions, and practices are to be brought into daily life. As Thầy encourages us, "Now is the time to practice."

I. Buddhas and Bodhisattvas

1. Opening with Compassion

The heart-mind,
rising with the eyes,
perceives the Bodhisattva
and opens with compassion

I started practicing with the Buddha's teachings in 2005, during a very stressful period of life and with a deep sense of suffering, grief, and exhaustion. At first, I was merely looking for ideas and practices that would complement what I was already doing and help me cope with the difficulties I faced. But the Buddha's voice, carried through thousands of years and over thousands of miles, offered more than I had hoped. As I practiced, I found that I was no longer just surviving; my suffering was being transformed. At the beginning, it was simply the feeling of relief that chanting and meditating gave me from the near constant crash of difficult and painful circumstances. But, little by little, I began noticing that this peace went with me as I got up from the cushion and even stayed with me throughout the day. Insights and aspirations that, at first, mainly arose during practice now started to percolate through my daily tasks and routines. These small habits held a big importance. They were making space within me where I could nourish insight and grow in wisdom, compassion, and even joy.

Along the way, I encountered tales and images of bodhisattvas. These began as fragments, powerful glimpses into a path of joyful transformation. Even without knowing their full stories, I began to understand. One of the images that particularly moved me during this time was that of Quán Thế Âm Bodhisattva, the One who Hears the Cries of the World, riding a dragon across the ocean of suffering. I had turned toward Buddhism when I felt lost in a such a sea. I was working so hard to stay afloat, but it was taking more and more energy to just tread water. I stayed strong outwardly, but the waves were overwhelming, and I could feel my limits. In the image of Quan Âm riding those waves, offering help and relief, I recognized my own experience. The Bodhisattva embodied a way of being that moved me from helplessness and despair to a powerful practice of cultivating a wise compassion.

When I moved to southwest Missouri in 2010, I never expected to find a Buddhist community. And when I first made my way to Định Quang Temple in 2011, I had no idea of where this journey would go. But the next year, a familiar image greeted me. In the temple courtyard, a 17 foot tall image of Quán Thế Âm rises above the temple grounds. She stands on a lotus blossom. Fittingly, she is the first sight that meets the eye when visiting the temple. Her right hand, with the ring finger meeting the thumb, offers a gesture of refuge and blessing, while her left hand holds a vase filled with the dew of compassion.

Even now when I look up at Bồ Tát Quán Thế Âm, I am reminded of the powerful compassion she embodies as she rides the waves of birth and death, of pain and suffering, to offer compassion to all who are drowning. I would later find this very image in **chapter 25 of the Lotus Sutra**:

> "... if you are cast adrift in a mighty Sea,
> surrounded by hydras, sea-nymphs and devil whales,
> Abide in Avalokitesvara and the shallows shall appear."

One of the most frightening parts of my own experience of being adrift in that sea of suffering was that I was losing touch with my capacity for kindness and compassion. My desperation increased with my difficulties, and my confidence that I could remain faithful to my own convictions and aspirations began to dwindle. That upward glance became a symbol of how compassion could still blossom within me. Sometimes, when we tread life's rough waters, all we can feel are the crushing waves and the fear of drowning. Looking up, seeing the visage of Quan Âm, I could remember that compassion was possible, even in the worst circumstances. I could receive this precious gift, and I could offer it in turn to both myself and others.

In this moment of this transformation, we are no longer drowning or even treading water. We are riding the waves.

Reflect:

- When is it more difficult for you to experience compassion? When does your heart-mind open more naturally and easily to compassion?

- Can you recall a time when you experienced compassion in an unexpected way, whether giving or receiving it, or when it was needed the most? How did that experience change your understanding of compassion?

- What people, stories, or symbols have embodied compassion, and helped open your own heart-mind to it?

- How and why is compassion important in your own spiritual life?

Practice:

- Keep a compassion journal. Each day, make a note of

at least one time when you offered or received an act of compassion.

- Volunteer at an organization that provides some compassionate service.

- Place a reminder of Quán Thế Âm Bodhisattva, such as a picture or statue, where you will see it each day. Pause and recite a simple aspiration, such as: “May my heart open to compassion this day, both to offer and receive it.”

2. "Not until the hells are emptied..."

Uttering the Great Vow,
Kṣitigarbha understands:
all obstacles will be overcome.

Walking the Bodhisattva way, we understand:
the six paramitas suffuse the six realms;
no realm or being will be abandoned.

During that stressful season in the early 2000s, I lived in rural Missouri, providing community programming and pastoral care. In addition to the familiar challenges, our communities were reeling from the emerging methamphetamine crisis. By 2004, Missouri led the nation in meth lab busts, with most of the drugs being produced in home labs. There was a great deal of shame around the problems, too. I remember one woman confidentially asking for help, looking for support for her granddaughter. She was waiting for me outside of my office on a crisp evening in October. We cried together as she told their story, the wind stinging our faces as evening fell. I shared as many resources as I could with her, recommended some treatment options, and encouraged her to seek support from others in the community experiencing these challenges. But this was too much; she recoiled and stammered, "Nobody can know about this; it would devastate the family!"

She was not alone, but the shame could be hidden only so long, as the need quickly outpaced the resources available in our little towns. Overwhelmed and uncertain, many people seemed to find it more comforting to avoid the problems than address them, pretending the suffering did not exist. My ongoing work, focused on family conflict, recovery resources, and spiritual care for marginalized members of the community, continued to be both vitally necessary and surprisingly controversial. We did our best to work together, as needs continued to grow. But I could feel my own wellbeing getting stretched thin; the spiritual disciplines that had sustained me were no longer adequate. The most pressing question was increasingly becoming: how can I practice in such a way that I can engage with suffering (inside and around me) with honesty, openness, compassion, and wisdom, without succumbing to apathy, rage, or despair? I felt increasingly frustrated at those who did not support our attempts to offer care to those who needed it and decreasingly hopeful that our efforts would make a difference.

The story of Kṣitigarbha was exactly what I needed in

that time of despair, with his vow that "Not until the hells are emptied will I become a Buddha." His presence made it possible for flowers to bloom even in the hell realm, and his unwavering commitment and confidence meant that he could be present with even the most overwhelming suffering. The possibility of that kind of presence spoke exactly to my situation and gave me hope. Previously, I had only studied bodhisattvas in an academic setting. Now, I began to understand not only their power and beauty, but how that power and beauty could translate into my own life and community. My heart resonated with the Great Vow, and I returned to my work with renewed energy - and hopefully with more insight and wisdom.

When I sat to write the mindfulness verse for Kṣitigarbha in 2022, I returned to chapter one of ***The Sutra on the Original Vows and the Attainment of Merits of Kṣitigarbha Bodhisattva***. Countless Buddhas and Bodhisattvas from infinite worlds gathered, celebrating the wisdom and power that guided beings to the end of suffering and paying homage to Shakyamuni Buddha. With this joy, the Buddha smiled, beams of wisdom and compassion radiating from him. This radiance filled space with the sounds of the six paramitas: generosity, virtue, patience, energy, concentration, and wisdom.

The image of Kṣitigarbha walking the hell realms appeared to me as a reverberation of those qualities, echoing through and filling every realm. The Bodhisattva not only reminds us that our Awakening is bound up together; he gives us a path to walk that embodies this profound insight and transformation. We understand that all beings, no matter their shortcomings or sufferings, have the capacity to awaken – and will. So, like Kṣitigarbha, we keep walking.

Reflect:

- Recall when *someone supported you* during an especially stressful time. How did that change your experience of suffering?

-Recall when *you supported someone else* during an especially stressful time. How did that change your experience of suffering?

-Kṣitigarbha's vow did not have an expiration date. How do you relate to suffering when change does not come quickly or easily?

-How does the image of a bodhisattva abiding in hell impact your understanding of Buddhist practice? What might Kṣitigarbha's vow mean in your own life?

Practice:

- Practice with the paramitas. Each day, choose a different quality: generosity, virtue, patience, diligence, concentration, and wisdom.

- How does that paramita empower you in bearing with great suffering?
- How does it relate to bringing about an end of suffering?
- What supports that quality in your own life?
- How does your practice of the paramita change your relationship with suffering?
- How does your practice open up the possibility of change for others?

- Place a reminder of Kṣitigarbha Bodhisattva, such as a picture or statue, where you will see it each day. Pause and recite a simple aspiration, such as: "May I and all beings be free from suffering; may our actions in thought, word, and deed incline to Awakening."

3. One Thousand Arms (part 1)

Before me with one thousand arms,
Avalokiteśvara manifests supreme giving.

Bowing with palms together,
may kindness and wisdom
be in perfect harmony.

Avalokiteśvara with 1,000 arms is another manifestation of Quan Âm Bodhisattva. The image is inspired by many texts and has inspired countless people across times and traditions. Each of the 1,000 hands has an eye in the palm, a reminder of a boundless and wise compassion that can both understand and relieve suffering. In the ***Śūraṅgama Sūtra***, the Bodhisattva describes how he can take whatever form the listener needs to clearly hear and understand the Dharma, opening a path to liberation. The list of these wonderful "transformation bodies" includes students, teachers, divine beings, warriors, royalty, elders, scholars, judges, monastics, laypeople, dragons, malicious spirits, and human beings of all ages and genders. He also "can take on different wonderful forms," with many heads and arms. Underlying this diversity is the undivided mind. The Buddha points out that these "wonderful forms" do not truly differ from one another, and no one path is superior or inferior to another, because each form is an embodiment of the Buddhas' liberating wisdom and compassion. In this spirit, the Buddha inquires which method is best suited to support Ananda in the path, "so that he can awaken to it and which one is easy of achievement, for the benefit of living beings … ."

Here, then, is one lesson in the one thousand arms: we encounter the Dharma in a multitude of ways, and our practice is to find a path that best suits us and supports one another in cultivating the Bodhi Mind. This frees us from comparison; we cultivate understanding, rather than approval or disapproval. It also opens up boundless opportunities. Each moment meets us with some expression of the Dharma, if we are willing to listen. In what wonderful form can we hear the Dharma today? How will we meet the Bodhisattva and glimpse liberation in this moment? And more – what forms do our own lives take in the expression of the bodhisattva ideal? How might others encounter the Dharma when they encounter us?

In **the *Kāraṇḍavyūha Sutra*,** Avalokiteśvara enters the Avīci hell to bring compassion there. The guards are confused and terrified when they see giant lotus flowers blooming and raging fires transforming into pools of cool water. A giant pot, echoing with the sounds of wailing from the millions suffering inside it, splits open, opening a way to freedom. Yamarāja , the god of Death, decides to investigate, curious about what being could possibly have the power to do such an incredible thing. Finding Avalokiteśvara, he bows down and praises him as one with great power, who - with 100,000 arms, millions of eyes, and eleven heads – brightens even the darkest corners and so completely relieves suffering. Yamarāja proclaims that this Bodhisattva creates wisdom, bestows joy, and extinguishes the flames of hell.

The themes overlap in these texts, but in extinguishing hell, we clearly see the great power of Compassion. In this image of Avalokiteśvara with 1,000 arms, the traditional form shows the Bodhisattva with palms together, holding a wish-fulfilling jewel. Five other hands hold different implements, while 992 hands are opened and empty in the mudra of supreme giving. The many arms, eyes, and heads remind us that compassion is greater than our suffering. Even the god of Death and lord of Hell bows to this Bodhisattva. In fact, one of Yamarāja's praises is that Avalokiteśvara is the one who offers "the supreme boon" – liberation from all suffering and the Awakening of the Bodhi mind.

So, we remember: the Bodhisattva's hands and eyes are always open: both to receive – to be with us in – our suffering and to offer us compassion. Both are gifts. So many of us live in isolation, without hope that another being truly cares about what we are going through, let alone that someone can help relieve that suffering. The supreme giving of Avalokiteśvara is the gift of compassionate presence, even in our worst pain. And that gift is so supreme that even the god of Death wonders at the lotuses blooming in hell, and he bows down in praise.

Reflect:

- What wonderful forms have best communicated the Dharma to you? Have any of them taken you by surprise?

- Why is it important that sharing the Dharma can take on many forms? How might that impact how you relate to your daily life?

- What does the image of the fires of hell being transformed into pools of cool water with blooming lotuses mean to you?

- How does "supreme giving" connect with compassion?

Practice:

Many Buddhist artists have offered creative pathways to contemplate the bodhisattvas and cultivate wisdom and compassion. Take time this week to connect with several of these "wonderful forms" of Avalokiteśvara. For example, you may:

- Listen to and contemplate with a mantra dedicated to Avalokiteśvara, such as "Om Mani Padme Hum" or "Namo Avalokiteśvara." (Many recordings are available with free access online on platforms like YouTube.)

- Go to a temple, museum, or website to contemplate images of Avalokiteśvara and how they relate to offering compassion. (Many museums now upload art depicting the Bodhisattva, complete with descriptions.)

- Make your own creative offering. Set a mantra to music. Write a poem about compassion. Paint a scene of Avalokiteśvara transforming the Avici hell. Practice the mudras associated with his depictions. Arrange flowers as an offering to the Bodhisattva.

4. One Thousand Arms (part 2)

Before me with one thousand arms,
Avalokiteśvara manifests supreme giving.

Bowing with palms together,
may kindness and wisdom
be in perfect harmony.

This depiction of Avalokiteśvara with One Thousand Arms, the One who Looks with Compassion, has obviously resonated with humans across time, place, and culture. He is the object of both devotion and artistic creation, as well as the inspiration for practice, for countless people. But there is another part to this tradition that has connected with us in a different way. It answers the question, but *why* does Avalokiteśvara have one thousand arms and eyes?

The story is told in chapter four of **the *Mani Kambum***, a collection of Tibetan texts that were most likely written in the 12th and 13th centuries. These texts focus on Avalokiteśvara and a seventh century king, Songtsen Gampo, who was recognized as an emanation of the Bodhisattva. The chapter begins as we would expect, with Avalokiteśvara coming before Amitābha Buddha and vowing that all sentient beings will find liberation. Amitābha praises the Bodhisattva and declares that he will be the Bodhisattva's companion in fulfilling this vow. Avalokiteśvara then emanates six beams of light that fill the six realms, and the Bodhisattva vows to relieve the suffering of every kind of being in every realm he visits. We recognize this powerful, transformative compassion – and it works! The six realms are emptied, three times over.

And yet, despite this wondrous success, the Bodhisattva realizes that more beings are simply replacing those he guides to liberation. A realm emptied from suffering does not stay empty for long. The size of the task suddenly strikes him, and it is inconceivable. Avalokiteśvara becomes depressed and, being depressed, he gives up. If the liberation of all beings is so impossible, he thinks that perhaps he has done enough after all. Perhaps, now, his own peace and happiness - his own liberation - is enough. The insight that our personal well-being and liberation cannot be separated from our collective well-being and liberation is - temporarily - forgotten.

However, one of his vows was that, if he should abandon even one sentient being, he would split into pieces. And this is exactly what happens. In the moment that he gives up on fulfilling his vow, Avalokiteśvara fractures. He suffers unbearable pain and utters "a woeful sound." But Amitābha Buddha remains a partner in compassion and gathers all the fragments. He refashions the Bodhisattva with eleven heads, one thousand arms, and an eye in each hand. Amitābha then gives him a mantra: *Om Mani Padme Hum*. Its six syllables correspond to liberation from the six realms. "Hold it," he counsels the renewed Bodhisattva. "Repeat. Perfect everything."

It is a story of aspiration, depression, brokenness, restoration, and transformation. It is a story essential for the cultivation of compassion, a wisdom that helps bring balance and harmony to our practice. We recognize ourselves here. We know the feeling of watching our most compassionate, skillful aspirations tested by exhaustion. We have felt the elation of giving and receiving compassion smashed to pieces by recognizing the complexity of what is left to be done. We have tasted the bitterness of depression when our best efforts are met with just more of the same, with no decrease in suffering. And we have heard a similar voice in our own heads – "what good is a bodhisattva vow? Wouldn't it be best to give up?"

What insight there is in hearing that a bodhisattva of great power became overwhelmed and depressed! And what understanding there is in seeing the response! Amitābha Buddha said that he also relied "on an aspiration like this" for his own Enlightenment, and that is why he wanted to be Avalokiteśvara's companion in the task. Amitābha *knew*, and he held compassion for Avalokiteśvara. The Bodhisattva's failure was met with kindness instead of condemnation. And rather than being cast aside as inadequate, Avalokiteśvara was given what he needed to fulfill his vow. These are lessons for us, too, in how we treat ourselves and one another, as we work together to create communities where kindness and wisdom are in perfect harmony.

Reflect:

- What is the significance of the story of Avalokiteśvara splitting into pieces? How does this connect with your own experience?

- How does Amitābha Buddha's response to Avalokiteśvara embody wisdom and compassion?

- Why is the mutual support of wisdom and compassion essential for walking the bodhisattva path?

- What might the image of one thousand arms mean for us today as a community of practitioners?

Practice:

- Visualize the story of Avalokiteśvara, contemplating

each of the main aspects. Chant one of the Bodhisattva's mantras at each stage:

- Aspiration (making the bodhisattva vow);
- Action (bringing liberation to each of the six realms);
- Depression (becoming discouraged at how much work is left to do);
- Giving up (splitting into pieces);
- Renewal (receiving compassionate help that restores and transforms);
- Fulfillment (returning to and accomplishing the bodhisattva vow).

- Journal about your experiences of compassion from multiple perspectives.
  - When have you felt discouraged like Avalokiteśvara, your compassion overwhelmed by suffering in or around you?
  - When have you acted like Amitābha Buddha, helping someone (perhaps even yourself) renew themselves?
  - When have you found a renewed ability to fulfill your aspiration?

- Place a reminder of 1,000 arms Avalokiteśvara, such as a picture or statue, where you will see it each day. Pause and recite a simple aspiration, such as: "May all who vow to embody compassion have everything they need to fulfill this aspiration."

5. All Obstacles Disappear

Perceiving the boundless ocean of merit,
Samantabhadra holds nothing for himself.

Jeweled lotus flowers fall like rain;
all obstacles disappear.

For most of my life, I've lived inland, among streams and lakes. I visited the Pacific and Atlantic Oceans once each as I grew up; both were special occasions. I then had the joy of living near oceans in both northern California, USA, and later in Cambodia. Although I love both, there is a different feeling between dangling my feet in an Ozarks' stream and wading into the waters of an ocean that stretch across the entire horizon. Having felt the immensity of that expanse certainly gives a more profound meaning to the image of the vast ocean of suffering that we glimpsed when reflecting on Quan Âm.

But this same image – the unfathomable size and power of an ocean – is flipped in other Buddhist scriptures and stories. While an ocean of suffering captures for us the experience of being overwhelmed, swallowed up, and left frantically hoping for shore by the hardships of life, the ocean of merit captures for us the boundless potential for wise and compassionate action. In the ***Practices and Vows of Samantabhadra Bodhisattva***, it is the merits and virtues of the Buddhas that are infinite. Samantabhadra explains that, if each atom in the universe represented a kalpa of time (about 16 million years), there still wouldn't be enough time to proclaim the boundless virtues of the Buddhas.

That boundlessness arises from the Ten-fold Paramita, the gateway to the Other Shore and basis of bodhisattva practice. Each of the ten practices flow from the first, to pay homage to all Buddhas. Moving through the aspirations, the practitioner grows in understanding and cultivation of the path. The more we understand what the Buddhas and their Awakening means, the more the heart-mind itself inclines to Awakening. There is no need for coercion, for example, when it comes to honestly recognizing and letting go of the unwholesome acts that hold us back, or from recognizing and celebrating the wholesome acts of others. The heart-mind opens with such generosity that it cannot view anyone as beyond the reach of this wisdom and compassion, including ourselves.

'I'll be a doctor for anyone who is sick,' the Bodhisattva of Great Action proclaims. 'I'll guide anyone who has lost their way. I'll make sure the poor find hidden treasures. All Buddhas hold this Great Heart in common. This Great Compassion brings forth the Bodhi-heart, and the Bodhi-heart brings forth Enlightenment.' He compares it to a huge tree in the desert. Even if no water is in sight, the roots go down deep, and the tree still flourishes with leaves, flowers, and fruit.

This all leads to the tenth and greatest aspiration, to dedicate these merits to all beings - that all of us together, without exception, will realize the Bodhi Mind. So, while the suffering of the six realms is great, this practice is up to the task. If "space is boundless," Samantabhadra says, "so also is my homage." If suffering arising from greed, hatred, delusion, and the like is boundless, so are the wholesome qualities that arise through skillful acts of body, speech, and mind. And even when all the karma and all the suffering of all beings comes to an end, this Heart of Great Compassion never will. This brings us back to the first vow; for when we act with the Heart of Great Compassion for all beings, that is the greatest homage we can offer to the Buddhas.

In **the *Lotus Sutra***, Samantabhadra's arrival is greeted with music and a gentle rain of jeweled lotus flowers. Countless bodhisattvas accompany him. He vows to protect all who take up that teaching and assures them they are planting "**deep roots of good merit**." We all have different experiences. For some of us, it is much easier to see the vast ocean of suffering than it is to see the boundless ocean of merit. But Samantabhadra's vows offer a pathway to train our actions of body, speech, and mind, and to find for ourselves that the Heart of Great Compassion is indeed more than enough: to bring about an end of every suffering and to bring forth the Bodhi Mind in every being. The roots go deep. The water is there. The practice is possible. Samantabhadra's vow includes me, a blossom on a mighty tree of Great Compassion. I, too, vow to cultivate it.

Reflect:

-Call to mind both images: the ocean of suffering and the ocean of merit. How do you relate to each? How do the two images relate to each other?

-Samantabhadra is called the Bodhisattva of Great Action. What are some ways in which his vows reflect that name?

-How does the analogy of the Great Tree provide both hope and guidance for cultivating the bodhisattva path, even in difficult conditions?

-Why is it that, when we act with the Heart of Great Compassion for all beings, that is the greatest homage we can offer to the Buddhas?

Practice:

-Contemplate the ten vows made by Samantabhadra Bodhisattva. How does (or might) each vow find expression in your life? In what ways does each vow connect back to the first, paying homage to all Buddhas?

-In order to glimpse the boundless ocean of merit even in difficult circumstances, consider using the "What Went Right" practice. Being careful not to minimize, deny, or repress suffering, reflect on the following question: "What had to go right in order for me to notice what went wrong?"

-Another version of this "What Went Right" practice is to bring your attention to some relationship, object, or experience that you may take for granted. For example, if you enjoy the benefit of access to clean drinking water: "What had to go right in order for me to be able to assume this water was safe to drink?"

-Place a reminder of Samantabhadra Bodhisattva, such as a picture or statue, where you will see it each day. Pause and recite a simple aspiration, such as:

May I and all beings bring forth
the Heart of Great Compassion.

6. The Entrance Opens

Mañjuśrī wields the scepter
that cuts through all dualities.

Beyond syllables and sounds,
the entrance opens.

Cultivating the Heart of Great Compassion is a powerful and beautiful aspiration, transforming all actions of body, speech, and mind into the Great Action of a bodhisattva. But the aspiration can easily get lost while we navigate through this realm of suffering. We face complicated questions and bump into our limitations at every turn. It is sometimes a short distance between a vow of Great Compassion and the shattered form we encountered with Avalokiteśvara. Mara's voice greets us at every turn, whispering: "Great Compassion is good and well in a perfect world, but you have to live *here*. It's not practical."

We can get lost in circles, perhaps a rut, bouncing between these skillful aspirations and the confusion of how to embody them in what we call the real world. We can get caught in our ideas of success and failure, or in others' praise and blame. But there is another possibility, a middle way beyond these binaries. For example, one of the most common questions I encounter when teaching meditation is, "am I doing it right?" We work together to move that question toward, "what happens when I do it this way?" Instead of a duality of good and bad, of approval and disapproval, we train the mind to pay attention, cultivate understanding, and choose actions with wisdom and compassion. We turn through our practice in spirals, passing through these lessons again and again, but deeper (or higher) at each turning. This isn't a rut; this is a ramp.

Our Gentle Friend in this path is Mañjuśrī, wielding the scepter of wisdom to help cut a path through our ignorance and free us from its inevitable suffering. In a chapter of **the *Vimalakīrti Sutra***, "The Dharma-Door of Nonduality," Vimalakīrti invites the many bodhisattvas who have gathered around to each give their explanation of how one goes about entering that gate of nondualism. One by one, they name a pair that forms a dualism and how to transcend it. The list covers birth and death; "I" and "mine"; defiled and pure; good and evil; blame and praise; created and uncreated; the realm of birth and death and nirvana; Enlightenment and ignorance; sense base and their objects; self and other; dark and light; correct and incorrect; true and false; and more. Mañjuśrī replies that entering the gate of nondualism is not the same as thinking about or explaining it. It's a direct experience that transcends questions and answers. The Bodhisattva is still pointing to the thing itself, but he doesn't name a dualism here, except for (perhaps) the dualism of words and no-words.

He then turns to Vimalakīrti and says, 'now it's your turn; what do you have to say about this?' And Vimalakīrti remains silent. He embodies Mañjuśrī's wisdom, opening the gate beyond syllables and sounds. In the sutra, Mañjuśrī sighs and speaks in reply, announcing that Vimalakīrti's silence – not a word! – is the true way here. This announcement is for our benefit, so that there is no confusion, lest we think that Vimalakīrti is silent because he doesn't understand or doesn't have something to say. In fact, words and no-words are not at odds. The chapter ends by noting that 5,000 of the bodhisattvas, upon hearing this chapter preached, entered that Dharma door of nonduality.

Teaching the Dharma is a gift, and the Bodhisattvas' descriptions help us glimpse just how steeped we are in dualistic thinking. These pairs surround us, are within us, and we carry them with us wherever we go. Hearing this list helps us both to understand how saturated our minds are with these opposing pairs, and to then understand that each moment can be a gateway to insight and wisdom that frees us from their ignorance. Each time a duality comes into awareness, we can yield ourselves to Mañjuśrī's sword. In the case of Vimalakīrti, we see this in action. After hearing all the descriptions of nondualism, he embodied it. His silence was not in opposition to the wise words spoken by the Bodhisattvas. Mañjuśrī recognized that the silence was the manifestation of wisdom - and offers to us the same opened door.

Reflect:

-What are some of the prominent dualities that you encounter? What makes them compelling to the mind?

-In our Buddhist practice, how might shifting the question from, "am I doing it right?" toward, "what happens when I do it this way?" help support the cultivation of wisdom and compassion?

-How is nondualism an expression of the Buddha's Middle Way?

-Why was Vimalakīrti's silence an embodiment of entering the Dharma door of nondualism?

Practice:

-Return to the analogy of Buddhist practice as a spiral. Contemplate how your own practice has included returning to and moving through certain lessons in new ways. What growth becomes clearer through this lens?

-Intentionally bring the question, "what happens when I do it this way?", into your practice. Choose a formal meditation activity (e.g., choosing your posture in meditation) or everyday routine (e.g., washing the dishes) and bring your attention to it in an open, curious, kind, and grateful way. If you notice a dualism arise (e.g., "am I doing this right?"), pause and reconnect with your openness. You can use the question, "what happens when I do it this way?", to signal your return.

- Place a reminder of Mañjuśrī Bodhisattva, such as a picture or statue, where you will see it each day. Pause and recite a simple aspiration, such as: "May the scepter of wisdom cut through all greed, hatred, and delusion."

7. A Healing Presence

Medicine Buddha awakens in us
the aspiration to cultivate well-being
in the realm of pain, disease, and suffering.

May we live in such a way
that all beings are free from harm
and quickly find the path of liberation.

Many years ago, some friends were delighted to harvest young leeks growing in their spring garden, a perfect addition to a salad of early greens. Unfortunately, some of the bulbs were actually daffodils and our friends spent the day at the emergency room. Instead of a celebration of the end of winter, they celebrated surviving an accidental poisoning. It was an easy mistake, and it was shocking that it could have been a deadly one.

The power of poison, that something we consume

could then consume us, also makes it a potent metaphor in the spiritual life. The Buddha called greed, hatred, and delusion the Three Poisons. Two others are often added to this list: when delusion and greed mix, they arise as pride. When greed and hatred mix, they arise as jealousy. The Poisons are an effective shorthand for all the unskillful and harmful ways we act in body, speech, and mind. They sustain the suffering that fills our lives, communities, and cultures. This is also why these Three Poisons are at the center of Buddhist depictions of the wheel of life: a pig (delusion), rooster (greed), and snake (hatred) endlessly chasing and biting one another.

At its most basic level, a poison is something that can cause illness or death in a creature when ingested or absorbed. Looking through the lens of greed, hatred, and delusion, we can easily see how ill - how very poisoned - our world normally is. Many of us have become so accustomed to the poverty, war, and oppression that have characterized human existence, that it may sound outrageous to even imagine a world without them.

Gratefully, we turn to the Medicine Buddha and find a remedy. His twelve Great Vows point a way to retrain our heart-minds to the possibility of healing, well-being, and Enlightenment in this very world of suffering. The first vow opens the door to liberation, a beautiful aspiration that all beings can become like him: a presence for healing in this world. We do not need to be defined by the poisons inside and around us. We are each more than the worst things we've experienced; more than the suffering we've known or even caused. Right here, in this heart-mind and in this moment, there can be an openness to being healed and offering healing from greed, hatred, and delusion.

The second vow turns this aspiration into action: may all beings be empowered to act according to this wish. Similarly, the third vow makes sure we have every resource we need and "never want for anything." The fourth vow protects us from wrong views and the fifth protects us from wrong actions. These all provide us with a strong basis for being a healing presence in the world. And the point is well taken; how many of our own personal resolutions and collective movements for change get stalled right here?

But with such a foundation, we can more clearly see Medicine Buddha's vision. What world will come about by these vows? One without disability (sixth), illness (seventh), misogyny (eighth), wrong views (ninth), imprisonment and state-sanctioned violence (tenth), hunger (eleventh), and poverty (twelfth). It's an overhaul of the way things are: a transformation of greed, hatred, and delusion into generosity, kindness, and understanding in a way that transforms not only ourselves, but our communities and world.

The suffering that exists in this realm is often entrenched and intractable, so much so that it begins to feel inevitable, if not natural. With Medicine Buddha, we begin to understand that the suffering that arises from the three poisons can be healed and even prevented, as we transform those conditions. It is true that, in this world, we face sickness, aging, and death, but even much of this suffering can be reduced through skillful care. Practicing these Twelve Great Vows, Medicine Buddha reminds us that we can work together to create a world where poverty, violence, exploitation, discrimination, and oppression of any kind are no longer assumed. Everyone having what they need to live a full life can become normal. Generosity, kindness, and wisdom can become normal. In a world overwhelmed by the Three Poisons, we ourselves can become an antidote. With Medicine Buddha, we can be a healing presence in the world.

Reflect:

-Give examples of how you have encountered the Three Poisons in: your life, relationships, community, and broader culture. What does it mean for us that these poisons (and their related social illnesses) are so common?

-What are some of the ways that the illnesses and disabilities we experience in our bodies are connected to the larger challenges we experience in our society?

-How do the first five vows of Medicine Buddha provide a strong basis for being a healing presence in the world?

-Why is it important for Medicine Buddha's first vow

to be that all beings become like him?

-Which of Medicine Buddha's vows resonate the most with you as a vision that embodies wellbeing and Awakening for all beings? How are they related to the urgent needs for healing of our own society?

Practice:

-Call to mind a community program, especially one that you support or with whom you volunteer. Contemplate how your actions are related to personal, interpersonal, community, and/or cultural healing.

-Recite the Medicine Buddha mantra. Ask your teacher for support, or chant along with a recording (many are available online for free). *Note:* Your temple may follow a specific tradition. For example, in Vietnamese, we chant: Nam Mô Dược Sư Lưu Ly Quang Vương Phật .

- Place a reminder of Medicine Buddha, such as a picture or statue, where you will see it each day. Pause and recite a simple aspiration, such as: "May all beings have everything they need to enjoy wellbeing and walk the path of generosity, kindness, and wisdom."

8. Illuminating the Land of Bliss

Compassion and Power together,
like Sun and Moon,
illuminate the Land of Bliss.

With Amitābha, they welcome us
to the Pure Land of the here and now.

You do not have to spend much time at the temple before you hear the recollection of a Buddha's name, especially "Nammô A Di Đà Phật." We use it to greet one another, say thank you, say goodbye, express care and compassion, and practice Buddha name recitation. The meaning, "Homage to the Buddha of Infinite Light," is an evocation of Amitābha Buddha. We recite the names of other Buddhas and Bodhisattvas, especially Shakyamuni Buddha ("Nam Mô Bổn Sư Thích Ca Mâu Ni Phật"), but our remembrance of A Di Đà Phật is constant. This reflects our tradition's practice of both Zen (Thiền) and

Pure Land Buddhist traditions.

In the Buddha Hall, three statues in particular connect us to the Pure Land practice: Amitābha Buddha is joined by Kuan Yin (Quan Âm) and Mahāsthāmaprāpta (Đại Thế Chí). These two Bodhisattvas bring together the power of compassion and the power of wisdom, respectively. Mahāsthāmaprāpta's name literally means "Great Strength." By the Bodhisattva's own description in **the *Śūraṅgama Sūtra***, that strength arose through the recollection of the Buddha, "with all my thoughts concentrated," opening the way to enlightenment. This is why, he explained, "I help all living beings of this world to control their thoughts by repeating the Buddha's name so that they can reach the Pure Land." (191)

The "all" in "all living beings" is especially important. Part of what makes the recollection of a Buddha so wonderful is its accessibility. A Buddha's name can be recited by anyone in any circumstance. In terms of practice, it's less of a shortcut and more of a direct path. Some teachers have compared it to a beetle that chews its way out of the side of a bamboo pole, rather than chewing through the stick's entire length. The practice is also flexible: we can cultivate recollection of a Buddha by reciting a Buddha's name, visualizing a Buddha, gazing on a Buddha image, and remembering a Buddha's qualities. Why is this so effective? The Buddhas and Bodhisattvas are constantly aware of unawakened beings, understanding that all beings "are of the same substance." But the unawakened struggle to remember and fall into heedlessness. We "renounce the roots while we grasp at the branches," lost in greed, hatred, and delusion. When we remember the Buddhas and Bodhisattvas, we also remember our own (and others') capacity for Awakening and the path of wisdom and compassion.

Over time, the practice goes deeply within, transforming our heart-minds. Pure Land teachings emphasize the cultivation of sincerity, faith, and the aspiration to be reborn in the Pure Land. Its broad vision is compelling, assuring Awakening. **The Venerable Thích Thiên Ân** described it as a place where "Everything ... teaches the Dharma." The birds sing Dharma songs, "the rivers hum sutras," and "flowers blossom in harmony with the blossoming of wisdom." All the conditions support the cultivation of wisdom and compassion. "In the Pure Land everything is a stepping stone on the way to Perfect Enlightenment."

And this insight brings the benefits of the practice into the here and now. One day, Thầy and I were visiting a local business office regarding some construction bids. The waiting area was filled with taxidermized hunting trophies of deer, turkeys, and fish. Thầy turned and asked, "Are they real?" When I nodded yes, he bowed to each of them in turn, compassionately reciting, Nammô A Di Đà Phật. Witnessing his sincerity, faith, and wise compassion was a powerful reminder that, with consistent practice, this simple recitation takes on a depth we previously could not imagine.

The more we are in touch with this vision, the more we understand what conditions make such a Pure Land possible. When we sing Dharma songs, we start to hear the Dharma from the birds. When we recite sutras, we start to hear the rivers hum them. When we cultivate wisdom, we recognize the wisdom of the flower. And more and more of our experiences become steppingstones on the path to Awakening. The wisdom and compassion of Amitābha's Pure Land can then shine from us. Venerable Thiên Ân described this as the Buddha's radiant light "growing larger and larger and brighter and brighter until it merges with our own inner light." And it offers to us a path by which "this world will become transformed into the Pure Land, this Samsara become Nirvana, and all the bliss and purity of the Western paradise become realized in the here and now of everyday life." Nammô A Di Đà Phật.

Reflect:

-Why is Amitābha Buddha accompanied by the Bodhisattvas of Compassion and Wisdom?

-What is the significance of Mahāsthāmaprāpta's name, especially in light of the path he took to Enlightenment?

-What are some ways that Pure Land practice embody inclusiveness and accessibility?

-How does contemplating Amitābha's Pure Land support the ideal that "this world will become transformed ... in the here and now of everyday life"?

Practice:

-Read and contemplate the vows of Amitābha Buddha. Which vows especially resonate with you? How can this support your practice?

-Read and contemplate a Pure Land sutra, mantra, and/or teaching. Ask your teacher to help you find suitable texts to support your study and practice.

-Place a reminder of Amitābha Buddha, Kuan Yin, and Mahāsthāmaprāpta (the Three Sages of the Western Pure Land), such as a picture or statues, where you will encounter them each day. Use this reminder as an opportunity to practice Buddha name recitation.

9. The Lotus' Radiant Bloom

A beam of sunlight travels countless miles
before awakening the lotus' radiant bloom.

Well-traveled through countless lives,
insight awakens Shakyamuni's radiant mind.

As far as we know, light can travel indefinitely. Moving at 186,000 miles per second, light can potentially travel 5.88 trillion miles in a single year. Scientists have even used redshift measurements to show that light can travel at least 15 billion light years before it drops below the visible spectrum. Sunbeams that light up our planet need only travel about 93 million miles before they arrive and help a lotus bloom. These numbers are so large that they are basically beyond human comprehension – which is exactly the point. Most sunlight doesn't find a lotus flower, but even the rays that do must travel further than we can imagine. Such a practically endless journey is a fitting metaphor for the path of Enlightenment before the Buddha set the wheel of the Dharma in motion.

That Shakyamuni Buddha taught about Amitābha Buddha and the Pure Land reminds us that the Buddhas know well the benefit of having a direct path to the end of suffering. In **the *Mahāparinibbāna Sutta*,** Shakyamuni Buddha reminded Ananda that "you and I have wandered and transmigrated for such a very long time." There was an inevitability to that wandering because, as the Buddha pointed out, it was all "due to not understanding and not penetrating four noble truths". Similarly, the metaphor of the ocean of suffering often makes an appearance when the Buddha teaches about rebirth. In **the *Assu Sutta***, the Buddha asks a poignant question about the painful realities of human existence:

> "No first point is found of sentient beings roaming and transmigrating, shrouded by ignorance and fettered by craving. What do you think? Which is more: the flow of tears you've shed while roaming and transmigrating for such a very long time—weeping and wailing from being united with the unloved and separated from the loved—or the water in the four oceans?"

His listeners wisely answer that their tears could overflow the oceans. In **another passage**, the Buddha invites his listeners to consider all the blood that has been shed in the course of being butchered as animals and executed as criminals. And again, the spilt blood is "more than the water in the oceans." In both cases, the Buddha emphasized that: "This is quite enough for you to become disillusioned, dispassionate, and freed regarding all conditions." For countless ages, beings have been caught, just like this: desperate for relief from suffering, but repeating the same actions that produce that suffering. Seeing this clearly, the heart-mind has a sense of "this is quite enough." And once a path was laid out by the Buddha, we no longer had to endlessly trudge and travel through numberless rounds of suffering. In **the Buddha's words**, "But now that these truths have been seen, / the conduit to rebirth is eradicated."

This is an example of two qualities that the Buddha extolled. *Samvega* is the feeling of exhaustion, disillusionment, or disenchantment we find with the enormity of suffering, along with both a sense of our own complicity in getting caught in that foolish cycle and an urgency to find our way through and out of it. By itself, *samvega* is wasted on our despair, nihilism, hedonism, asceticism, or any other strategy we might use to deny or ignore the ocean of suffering. In the end, we commonly use these coping strategies to justify the unwholesome acts that ultimately perpetuate the endless flow of tears and blood. But hearing and practicing the Four Noble Truths channels *samvega* into *pasada*, a sense of clarity and confidence. In Buddhist practice, this confidence is in the Four Noble Truths. The Buddha's teaching offers a path that transforms *samvega* into *pasada* and suffering into wisdom and compassion, leading to Awakening.

And just as sunlight opens the lotus blossom, the Dharma opens the heart-mind. **The Buddha described** its wondrous capacity in this way: “This mind, mendicants, is radiant. But it is corrupted by passing corruptions. ... This mind, mendicants, is radiant. And it is freed from passing corruptions. A learned noble disciple truly understands this.” Knowing that we can pass beyond the futility of a fruitless path, we enter the freedom of *samvega* that knows *pasada*: “This is quite enough for you to become disillusioned, dispassionate, and freed regarding all conditions.” Practicing the Buddha’s teachings, we can know that this mind, too, is radiant.

Reflect:

-What role did contemplating the oceans of tears and blood play in understanding and practicing the Buddha’s teachings?

-How is the insight of *samvega* connected with the teachings on rebirth?

-How is the insight of *pasada* connected with the teachings of the Four Noble Truths?

-Regarding the radiant mind, what is it that the learned disciple understands?

Practice:

-Reflect on the suffering that has plagued human history, from the ancient past to today's headlines. In what ways does it demonstrate the Buddha's points about the oceans of tears and blood? How has greed, hatred, and delusion repeatedly corrupted the radiant mind?

-Contemplate *samvega* and *pasada* in your own life. When have you felt this disenchantment, along with a sense of your own complicity and urgency to find your way out of it? How have the Buddha's teachings empowered you to move through that feeling into a sense of clarity and confidence in your practice? How does this transform suffering into wisdom and compassion?

-Plants respond to their environment, especially sunlight and precipitation, to grow and bloom at the most ideal time. Photoreceptors have proteins that respond to the light and trigger a molecular process responsible for blooming. This can be a metaphor for our own experience of insight. The practice trains the mind to be a sensitive receptor to insight, setting in motion a transformation that allows wisdom and compassion to blossom.

Visualize your mind as a lotus plant, awaiting the light of insight. Imagine the journey of a ray of light through countless miles, finally resting on this lotus plant. Watch the stems produce buds that then bloom. Finish by resting in gratitude for the insights that have brought you to this path of practice, gratefully resolving to be "freed from passing corruptions."

10. The Dharma Treasure

The Dharmapālas, knowing
the immeasurable value of the Teachings,
pledge themselves to guard this place
and all who practice.

May I also abide in mindfulness
of the Dharma treasure,
with grateful attention and fierce resolution
to walk the Bodhisattva path.

Images of Dharma protectors adorn the outer walls of our temple, along with a shrine to Skanda within the Buddha Hall. Their (often) ferocious countenances and drawn swords embody a fierceness that sometimes assures - and sometimes intimidates. Yet this fierceness is rooted in compassion and a dedication to protecting the Buddha's teachings and practitioners. While

Dharmapāla practices and emphases vary according to tradition, they all encourage us to reflect on how our Buddhist path connects with both a sense of protection and an awareness of what we trust and value.

To begin, the protectors remind us to take refuge in the Buddha, Dharma, and Sangha. They are *Dharma* protectors, after all. As **the *Dhammapada* teaches us**:

> "The gift of the teaching surmounts all other gifts;
> the taste of the teaching surmounts all other tastes;
> the joy of the teaching surmounts all other joys;
> the ending of craving surmounts all suffering."

In this same chapter, the Buddha offers us a stark contrast, reminding us that "When a person lives heedlessly, / craving grows in them like a parasitic creeper." As our practice deepens in kindness and insight, we better understand that our greed, hatred, and delusion offer no protection for us: "Whoever is beaten by this wretched craving, / this attachment to the world, / their sorrow grows, / like grass in the rain."

So, when we talk about the protection these Bodhisattvas offer, we should not get it confused with taking refuge in anything less than the Triple Gem. Remembering our lessons cultivating *samvega* and *pasada*, we understand that taking refuge in impermanent, changing conditions leaves us more vulnerable to suffering, not less. We cannot make ourselves impervious to suffering by simply "getting what we want," or by pretending that we do not want anything. Likewise, we cannot hide from the fruit of our actions of body, speech, and mind. The Dharma protectors are a powerful reminder that our greed, hatred, and delusion lock us into a cycle of suffering, but the Buddha's teaching gives us a path through and out. That's where our true safety lies.

This being the case, we are also invited to embody the fierce protection of the Dharmapālas in our own lives and for our own practice of the Dharma. A familiar encouragement is found in **the *Mettā Sutta***, where we are exhorted to **care for and protect the boundless heart**, full of kindness and goodwill, just like a mother cares for and protects her only child. This attitude naturally arises when we: first, take time to connect with the unlimited goodness of a path that skillfully and compassionately guides us out of suffering; and second, contemplate how precious and wonderful this opportunity to hear and practice like this truly is, especially in light of life's uncertainty and impermanence.

We also practice in this way as a gift to one another. In the *Mettā Sutta*, we are encouraged to consider how the wise would be impacted by our actions and to avoid things that bring harm: deceiving, despising, and wishing for bad things to happen to others. This is the letting-go aspect of this practice. Simultaneously, we increase the capacity – that boundless heart – to practice in a way that supports harmlessness and expresses itself through living simply, honestly, peacefully, with kindness and care. Again, this is an expression of the value of the Dharma and our commitment to practicing it. It requires our persistent, consistent effort, and it is worth that effort. The precepts and *vinaya* are, in this way, an aspect of the Dharma's protective qualities. They support us in matching our aspirations to treat the Dharma as the most valuable of gifts with our practice of those teachings. The strength of our ignorance, fueling greed, hatred, and delusion, may lead us to doubt that this is the case. The Dharma protectors offer the message to us in no uncertain terms: there is nothing more valuable than a path of practice that brings forth kindness and wisdom, inclining the heart to liberation.

Reflect:

-What is the meaning of the fierce or wrathful countenance in images of the Dharma protectors?

-The Dharma protectors invite us to reflect on where we find safety and protection amid uncertainties and impermanence. How do we recognize where we are taking refuge in our daily lives? How might that recognition help us on our path?

-In what ways can we reflect the role of Dharma protector when it comes to our own Dharma practice? How do we communicate the value of both the Buddha's teachings and the opportunity to cultivate wisdom and compassion in this life?

-The images of Dharma protectors greet us as we arrive at the temple. What is the purpose of this reminder? How can we encourage one another, and develop a safe place to deepen our practices, as a temple community?

Practice:

-Learn more about the Dharma protectors that are represented at your temple. What are their related stories, rituals, and practices?

-Contemplate the image of protection from the *Mettā Sutta*. Envision your boundless heart (the cultivation of goodwill, compassion, joy, and equanimity) as a baby, cradled in your arms. Connect with the awareness you feel of how precious that practice is and the sense of protection you feel for caring for and nourishing that practice. Note how your relationship with the practice is changed in this context of protection and care.

-Place a reminder of protection, such as a picture or statue, where you will see it each day. This could be an image of a Dharma protector, but it may also be an image of a parent or caregiver protecting a child, or an aspect of nature that you find communicates safety. Pause and recite a simple aspiration, such as: “May I and all beings find true refuge, a path that leads to the end of suffering.”

II. Practices

11. That Such Beauty Can Blossom

Entering the Buddha Hall,
I recognize the generosity and care
that sustains this place of practice.

The heart-mind brightens with gratitude
and quickly resolves to practice so that
such beauty can blossom in all places.

Entering the Buddha Hall is an embodied practice, bringing body together with thoughts and feelings. The way we enter reflects our awareness and aspirations. We are slowing down, joining intention with attention. Our intentions include a commitment to practice and to express respect and gratitude to the Triple Gem. Our attention is on how we express that gratitude and respect through actions of body, speech, and mind. We prepare by taking off our shoes and putting on a temple robe. We slow our walking pace. We stop and bow with palms together at the shrines to Avalokiteśvara with 1,000 Arms and to our lineage teachers. We bow again when we enter the hall and see the Buddha altar. We may offer incense and touch the earth. We find our place in the hall and stand or sit mindfully, feeling the support of this place, its beautiful customs, and its dedicated community.

For those of us who did not grow up in a Buddhist culture and tradition, this kind of reverence might feel uncomfortable at first. We may feel anxious about accidentally doing something incorrectly, or afraid that we do not know how to show respect. The opposite tendency may also arise, especially for those with a religious background that emphasized prohibitions of icons and images or, in other cases, that carried religious harm. When resistance arises, entering the Buddha Hall may feel confusing or overwhelming. What does it mean to be in the presence of these statues, paintings, and offerings? What does it mean if I bow, or if I do not bow? Facing the unknown, we might find ourselves asking: is this place emotionally and spiritually safe for me?

When they are present, we cannot skip over these anxieties; working with them becomes part of the practice of entering the Buddha Hall. Pause. Stop if you need to. Listen to your body; honor the anxiety, fear, or resistance. Understanding those experiences is a gift. With awareness, the possibility of acting intentionally returns. How can you respond to these feelings and needs with compassion and wisdom? This is how we practice the

Buddha's teachings. Give yourself permission to take the time and gain the experience you need to understand both yourself and the temple's traditions. Become curious; ask questions; tend to your heart-mind, including places that need healing.

But for others, entering the Buddha Hall immediately grants a feeling of wellbeing. Guests have often mentioned that entering the hall bathes them in peace, and some visit the temple simply to enjoy that feeling. This is welcomed and wonderful, but it is also not by accident. That peace exists only because of generous and skillful effort. Whenever we enter the Buddha Hall, we are benefitting from both a culture and a community that makes it possible. These practices – the beauty of the art; the careful tidiness; the fresh offerings of fruit and flowers; the careful attention to presentation; the architecture that invites bright light to scatter below high ceilings; even the simple presence of a meditation cushion – were developed, refined, and adapted across centuries and cultures, so that we could enjoy them today. Recognizing this, we feel a deep gratitude to the countless practitioners, most of them unnamed and forgotten, who nourished these traditions and passed them down. And we are grateful to everyone whose generosity and care sustains the Buddha Hall that we enjoy today. That generosity and care is itself a core practice of the Buddha's teachings.

We can feel the unfolding of this practice: preparing; entering the Hall; pausing and recognizing; experiencing and expressing gratitude; resolving to practice in response. We find this aspiration settling in our hearts to not only respect and enjoy the Buddha Hall in this moment, but to practice in a way that makes this kind of beauty and peace possible in every space we visit. And over time, as the Buddha nature blossoms within us, we can more naturally encounter the Dharma wherever we are.

Reflect:

- Do you remember the first time you visited a Buddha Hall? What were your reactions? How has your experience changed over time?

- Were there any customs that have either confused or interested you? Were you able to explore those customs and find out more?

- How do you now experience and express respect and gratitude when you practice entering a Buddha Hall?

- How does cultivating accessibility and inclusion at the temple relate to this practice?

Practice:

- Find at least one practical way that you can participate in the generosity and care that sustains the

Buddha Hall. This can include:

- donating money, supplies, decorations, or offerings;
- helping clean the Hall;
- volunteering to help with holiday preparations and cleanup;
- learning about the Buddhas, Bodhisattvas, and Dharma items in the Hall; and
- helping provide tours and welcoming guests.

- Set aside time to practice like this, both at the temple and, as possible, at your home.

- *Preparing*: choose an action that helps you pause, become aware, and connect with your intentions.
- *Entering the Hall*: offer a bow and then stand or sit mindfully, enjoying the present moment.
- *Pausing and Recognizing*: take time to notice what makes that moment possible, from teachers and friends, to everyone who supports the temple, to your own skillful effort and time.
- *Experiencing and Expressing Gratitude*: let your heart-mind settle on that feeling of appreciation and nurture it. Call to mind how you have benefited from your practice, how you've healed, grown, and been transformed. If appropriate, make offerings of incense, fruit, flowers, chants, or mantras.

- *Resolving to Practice and Sharing the Merit*: intentionally transform this gratitude into an aspiration to cultivate wisdom and compassion. Dedicate your practice to the wellbeing of specific people, or to the benefit of all beings.

12. The Earth Rises to Meet the Cushion

The earth rises to meet the cushion,
bearing witness to the present moment.

The Buddha's right hand
reaches downward;
I smile.

When we sit to meditate, we pause to become aware of the body. We take the time we need to adjust the posture, to pay attention and respond to the body with kindness and understanding. This allows us to connect with a sense of stability and balance in the body, neither rigid nor slouched. We make sure we are supporting the body, which allows the body to support the practice. We take special care to notice the parts of the body that touch the earth, whether it is our feet, knees, or sit bones. The body teaches us the sense of this physical groundedness, and we can learn to recognize a similar mental and emotional groundedness: balanced, stable, and at peace in the present moment.

This groundedness is a gift. It passes upward through the earth, into the cushion, chair, or bench, and into our bodies. I like to pause and cultivate gratitude for the Earth, feeling her stability supporting my practice. In this pause, I also feel deeply connected to the Buddha's own moment of Enlightenment, when he called upon the Earth to bear witness to his journey to Awakening. In chapter 21 of **the *Lalitavistara Sutra***, Siddhartha is sitting under the Bodhi tree, the Seat of Awakening, when Mara, the demonic lord of the realm of desire, tries to prevent him from attaining liberation. Mara tries several tactics, including accusing Siddhartha that there is no reason to believe he is worthy of Enlightenment because there is no witness to his spiritual journey. Whether to stir up doubt or to distract the Bodhisattva, attempting to lure him into debate, Siddhartha is undisturbed. He smiles and names the Earth as his witness. He then embraces Mara and his demonic horde with love and compassion. He lets his right hand reach down to gracefully touch the earth. 'The Earth supports every being and is impartial to all,' he says. 'She knows that I am not lying, and she can bear witness on my behalf.'

The goddess arises, shaking the earth, bows down before Siddhartha, and says, "You are right. Great Being, you are right." In the sutra, the demons run away in terror, like jackals running from a lion's roar. In the Thai version of the story, Earth wrings the waters from her hair, releasing a flood that washes Mara away. In both cases, it is a powerful story of the Buddha's Enlightenment and, in turn, of our deep connection with the Earth. Over billions of years, the Earth has witnessed and participated in the evolution of life. We have always depended on the Earth for everything we need; we depend on her still today. And when we die, our bodies return to the Earth. It is in this precious human life on this precious Earth that we have encountered the Dharma. This Earth, then, is where we practice; our actions of body, speech, and mind are done right here. The Earth is our witness.

The relative stability of the Earth also reminds us that we are impermanent, inconstant, and subject to change. Her long witness to change puts our lives into perspective. For example, I love walking in the Ozarks, and there is a special place in my heart for glades and hillsides with limestone outcrops. Even after all these decades, I still pause in wonder that I am on the floor of what used to be an inland sea, the result of millions of years of marine animals living and dying. And when the sea receded, layers of shale, limestone, and sandstone were left behind. How can I *not* remember that my life is but a brief moment, and that the Earth is a record of that brevity? In **the *Pabbatūpama Sutta*** (*The Simile of the Mountains*), the Buddha asks King Pasenadi what should be done when we realize that aging and death are crashing in on us like an avalanche. The king replies, "what can I do but practice the teachings, practice morality, doing skillful and good actions?" The Earth holds me accountable – tenderly, beautifully, but also insistently - to this urgency.

In this way and more, the Earth bears witness to the Buddha and his teachings, and many Buddhist traditions continue in Siddhartha's footsteps by practicing close to the Earth, in forests, caves, and out of the way places. We can maintain that spirit, wherever we practice, whether sitting, standing, walking, or lying down. We are following the example of the Buddha, feeling the support of the Earth to practice as we also cultivate wisdom and compassion. Calling to mind the Buddha's Awakening, we can offer the Bhumisparsha mudra, "touching the earth." And just as Siddhartha smiled in response to even Mara's fiercest attacks, confident in liberation, we can remember our own Buddha nature, and smile.

Reflect:

-What ways have you noticed that, if you support the body, the body can support the practice?

-When it comes to your own experiences of practice, have you noticed messages of doubt and debate, like those that Mara used? Have you noticed messages of affirmation and support, like those that the Earth used?

-Why is King Pasenadi's reply to the Buddha's

question about impermanence a skillful one?

-What Earth-related practices have you found supportive, whether practicing outside or bringing natural elements indoors?

Practice:

-Take time to explore how you meditate in different postures (sitting, standing, walking, and lying down). How can you make choosing or adjusting your posture an expression of kindness and understanding?

-Although we are never separate from the natural world, since we are part of it, our lives can easily become alienated from the Earth. Practice mindfulness either outside (e.g., sitting meditation under a tree) or by focusing on natural elements (e.g., making a flower or stone your object of meditation).

-Dedicate yourself to some expression of caring for and protecting the Earth, in gratitude for the Earth's support of the Buddha's Awakening and our own journeys of cultivating wisdom and compassion.

13. The Lotus Blossoms

From the mud, the lotus blossoms.
From the suffering, understanding blooms.

From the heart-mind, the delicate petals
of love and equanimity open,
offering their perfume.

The Buddha was staying along the shore of Gaggara Lake when **the Venerable Bahuna approached** and asked, "Sir, how many things has the Realized One escaped from, so that he lives unattached, liberated, his mind free of limits?" How many things? Perhaps the memory of those moments under the Bodhi Tree, when Mara assailed him and the Earth bore witness, filled his mind. Out of all the many, many things he had escaped, what would he name? His answer was ten: form, feeling, perception, choices, consciousness, rebirth, old age, death, suffering, and defilements. It is a list that contains all other lists, mapping a way out of the suffering that gives birth to suffering – like links in a chain. With the chain broken, the Tathagata was truly free.

"Suppose there was a lotus," the Buddha continued, sitting there on the shore of a lotus lake. "Though it sprouted and grew in the water, it would rise up above the water and stand with no water clinging to it. In the same way, the Realized One has escaped from ten things, so that he lives unattached, liberated, his mind free of limits." We don't get to know Bahuna's reaction (the sutta doesn't tell us), but this just opens the door for us to sit with the Buddha's words at our own lotus ponds.

When you do, you can observe that a lotus leaf has an amazing knack for staying dirt-free, even though they grow in muddy places. You can also observe that water will bead on the leaves and easily roll off. If you could get a microscopic view, you'd then find that a lotus leaf isn't smooth. It has a rough, porous surface made of wax crystals or tubules. The spaces between the tubules fill with air, so that anything resting on the lotus is touching more air than leaf. Dirt and water bind more easily to each other than to the leaves because dirt and water don't bind easily to air. And when the leaves move, even with a gentle breeze, the water and dirt roll right off. These super-hydrophobic properties are dubbed "the lotus effect" and have inspired the creation of water-repellent materials that mimic the leaf's structure. "Though it sprouted and grew in the water, it would rise up above the water and stand with no water clinging to it."

There's a picture here for all of us who are walking in the footsteps of the Buddha. A lotus leaf has a different way of relating to dirt and water than most things, just as the Buddha has a different way of relating to gain and loss, status and disgrace, praise and blame, and pleasure and pain. In **the *Lokavipatti Sutta***, the Buddha described the wise, mindful person as one who recognizes that these conditions keep spinning after the world, and the world keeps spinning after these conditions. But rather than getting consumed and caught, they understand that all these conditions are inconstant and unreliable. Spinning after them offers no end to suffering, just the dizziness of the endless cycle. The Buddha called that dizziness "welcoming and rebelling," constantly chasing after what we name as pleasant and running away from what we name as unpleasant. But for the wise, compassionate one, none of these conditions can cling to the Bodhi Mind any more than water and dirt can cling to a lotus leaf. "Desirable things don't disturb their mind, nor are they repelled by the undesirable."

In **the *Theragatha***, Venerable Udāyin praises the Buddha in just this way, as One who cut all the bonds, from the tiniest to the largest fetter. The Buddha was born here and lived in this world without clinging or longing, his concentration unbroken, "like a lotus in the water." The Buddha's path opens up a way of being in this realm of suffering without clinging to those things that bring about suffering. Wisdom and compassion create an openness for experiences to come and go, known fully but without clinging. That might sound impossible, but the lotus is right here to be our teacher. Changing our relationship with our experience, beyond welcoming and rebelling, we can grow like a lotus: out of the mud, through the water, without clinging to either; offering the sweet fragrance and beautiful bloom of wisdom and compassion.

Reflect:

-Why is the lotus leaf a good analogy for the Buddha's approach to understanding suffering and bringing about an end of suffering?

-Return to the list of eight conditions described in the *Lokavipatti Sutta.* How does each pair connect with the experience of spinning, or "welcoming and rebelling"?

-How does cultivating wisdom and compassion offer a Middle Way beyond that "welcoming and rebelling"?

-What connects this practice of going beyond "welcoming and rebelling" with the Buddha's list of the ten things the Realized One escaped?

Practice:

-If one is available, visit a lotus pond. Spend time in

both meditation and observation, contemplating the lotus leaf's properties and the Buddha's teachings. (Alternatively, contemplate using an image or description of a lotus.)

-Use "welcoming and rebelling" as a noting practice. As you go about your day, pay attention for when your heart-mind chases after some pleasant experience (welcoming), or runs away from an unpleasant one (rebelling). Cultivate a sense of how easy it is to spin after those conditions, and when you are most likely to do so.

-Contemplate the four pairs the Buddha named in the *Lokavipatti Sutta*: gain and loss, status and disgrace, praise and blame, and pleasure and pain. Identify a simple example for each condition. Calling each to mind in turn, contemplate how it is impermanent, inconstant, and subject to change. *Note:* especially when beginning this practice, choose examples that do not provoke a strong emotional response. This expression of compassion will support you in cultivating the necessary skills to work with more difficult experiences in the future.

14. Bowing to the Ancestors

Bowing to the ancestors,
I gratefully resolve to nurture
the skillful qualities I inherited from them.

Bowing to the ancestors,
I gratefully resolve to heal
the suffering I inherited from them.

Like too many of us, I don't have a strong sense of my larger family history or ancestry. There have been a few attempts at genealogy, especially on my father's side, but my knowledge has remained hazy. We had some traditions that linked us to our ancestors, such as decorating graves, but my personal connections were mainly with the relatives that lived to meet me. I remember, for example, traveling to visit my mother's grandmother several times a year when we also would pick berries, camp out on the river, and decorate graves. Some memories of those visits remain vivid, such as stepping into my great grandmother's house (the original room still had a dirt floor, but the modest addition had a wooden floor and even an electric light); listening to the mountain lions scream at night; running down the hill to the river to be greeted by a very surprised cottonmouth snake; eating fresh gooseberry pie with ice cream.

But I cannot tell you much about my great grandmother's life, or the lives of my other ancestors. My grandparents mostly died young, as well: my maternal grandfather before I was born; my paternal grandfather when I was a preschooler; my maternal grandmother during my freshman year of university; my paternal grandmother during my graduate studies. They were all gone before I even grew up. Still, I have a deep sense of connection with them. Gardens, for example, fill my senses when I think of them. We were barely removed from our rural, hillbilly days, and I spent a large amount of my childhood helping with the planting, weeding, picking, and preserving. Even past the harvest, there was work to do, such as tending the bowl of walnuts on the kitchen table. If you could sit to drink a cup of coffee, you could crack and pick.

When I think of my ancestors, I bow in gratitude for these wonderful gifts. I have inherited a joyful closeness to the earth; an appreciation of and skill in making music; a habit for generosity, kindness, and compassion for others; a diligent and steady commitment to hard work; a sense of faithfulness and loyalty; and a love and respect for learning. I especially witnessed these qualities in my parents, and I have a deep gratitude for them and for these gifts, which I know they received, cultivated, and handed down to me.

But also like too many of us, I inherited painful karmic patterns that live in and across generations, including the suffering that arises from poverty, domestic violence, abuse and neglect, and substance use disorders in my broader family and community. And because our world was suffused with the ignorance of bigotry, we internalized and enacted both the dominance and oppression that props up those systems. I saw quite clearly that people who were capable of love and care in some circumstances were also capable of indifference, hatred, and cruelty in others. I, too, carried scars from experiences that required years of attention, transforming woundedness into a practice of healing and growing.

From old memories to current relationships, Buddhist practice continues to be a vital part of this transformation, both where there is joy and where there is pain. When I think of my ancestors, I bow in gratitude for the opportunity to be part of that healing, to be a place where those karmic formations can be resolved. Honoring my ancestors requires this honesty; lying about the painful parts of our shared history only prolongs the suffering. I make room for both aspects: celebrating the wondrous gifts that support the aspiration to cultivate wisdom and compassion, inclining to Awakening; and healing the wounds, opening a way for us to move forward with greater peace, joy, and meaning.

We will return to these themes when we reflect on the Vu Lan (Ullambana) celebration. But the practice is with me every day. I bow to my ancestors, both biological and spiritual, remembering them with photos and honoring them with simple gifts of incense, candles, flowers, fruit, or tea. These simple acts reconnect me with my aspirations to practice. I realize that I could not exist without them, and I gratefully vow to make this precious human heart a place where all that is skillful, wholesome, and wise can thrive, and all that is unskillful, unwholesome, and harmful can heal.

Reflect:

-How does a connection with our ancestors support our practice? Or how does ignorance of or alienation from our ancestors impact our practice?

-Why is it important to include both aspects of our ancestral inheritance (skillful qualities and suffering) in our practice?

-What does it mean for each of us "to be a place where those karmic formations can be resolved"?

-We often describe our relationship with ancestors as

a continuation. How might this idea transform our relationship with our ancestors? With our descendants?

Practice:

-Take time to get in touch with your spiritual ancestors. Mindfully make a list of teachers, writers, mentors, caregivers, and others who have nurtured your spiritual life, across times and cultures. If you belong to a Buddhist temple or lineage, take time to learn about this history.

-Ask your teacher about ancestor ceremonies at your temple. These often take place at holidays, funerals, and special memorials. If possible, participate in one of these ceremonies.

-Set aside a space to honor your biological and spiritual ancestors. This can be as simple as hanging photographs on the wall, with a shelf for offerings like incense, candles, flowers, fruit, or tea. You may enjoy using a simple aspiration, such as this chapter's verse: "Bowing to the ancestors, I gratefully resolve to nurture the skillful qualities I inherited from them. Bowing to the ancestors, I gratefully resolve to heal the suffering I inherited from them."

15. Our Mutual Dependence

Happy is our mutual dependence:
householders offering requisites;
monastics offering the Dharma.

Happy is the purpose of this path:
crossing the flood of suffering,
arriving safely at the Other Shore.

Siddhartha Gautama's path to Awakening also connects with human economics and tensions between wealth and poverty. The Buddha described his upbringing as being "**extremely delicately nurtured**." As much of life as possible was arranged for his enjoyment and comfort, from the beauty of the lotus gardens to the luxuriousness of his clothing. He had three mansions, each especially designed for winter, summer, or rainy seasons. He was constantly attended by musicians for his entertainment and servants for his needs. In one detail, he noted that, "By day and by night a white canopy was held over me so that cold and heat, dust, grass, and dew would not settle on me." But Siddhartha eventually understood that all of this was a futile attempt that could not erase the realities of sickness, aging, and death, just as an umbrella could not erase the realities of heat, dust, grass, and dew. "When I reflected thus, my intoxication with youth, with health, with life, was completely abandoned."

So he traded opulence for austerity, taking up such an austere life that he drove himself nearly to death. Over-exerted and under-nourished, "**my vertebrae stuck out like beads on a string**, and my ribs were as gaunt as the broken-down rafters on an old barn." And yet this violence to his body and mind did not bring him any closer to Awakening: "this is as far as it goes, no-one has done more than this. But I have not achieved any superhuman distinction in knowledge and vision worthy of the noble ones by this severe, grueling work. Could there be another path to awakening?"

Transcending these tensions, Siddhartha's years of asceticism ended when he accepted a bowl of milk-rice pudding from a young woman named Sujata. Though his fellow mendicants were disgusted with the indulgence, that nourishing meal gave Siddhartha the strength he needed for his body to begin to recover and sustain his spiritual path. Sujata paid attention and recognized the opportunity to support Siddhartha's skillful aspirations with kindness and generosity. In turn, the newly awakened Buddha recognized the opportunity to support householders like Sujata by offering the Dharma with both actions and words. This is a beautiful picture of the path of practice, as well as a demonstration of how the Buddha's community would reflect the Middle Way.

The Buddha and his disciples would be neither princes nor ascetics. No, the monastic Sangha would not be caught by either trap, neither exploiting the generosity of householders by accumulating wealth nor harming themselves through spiritualizing the violent realities of poverty. Instead, they would be a community of practice that relied on the lay community for the basics of life: food, clothing, medicine, and shelter. Householders would make possible and receive the gift of the Dharma in words and deeds. Sangha and householders would live in mutual dependence, without coercion, guilt, or exploitation. Thanissaro Bhikkhu called this "**an economy of gifts**" that blossoms out of the faithful practices of everyone involved. The Buddha described this in the ***Bahukāra Sutta***:

> "Mendicants, brahmins and householders are very helpful to you, as they provide you with robes, almsfood, lodgings, and medicines and supplies for the sick. And you are very helpful to brahmins and householders, as you teach them the Dhamma that's good in the beginning, good in the middle, and good in the end, meaningful and well-phrased.

> And you reveal a spiritual practice that's entirely full and pure. That is how this spiritual path is lived in mutual dependence in order to cross over the flood and make a complete end of suffering."

When our teacher recently returned from India, he joyfully shared about visiting Bakraur village near Bodh Gaya. Tradition remembers this as Sujata's village, and a stupa there was dedicated over two thousand years ago in her honor. That simple, small gift of milk-rice set into motion an unbroken chain of generosity that extends all the way to us: householders sharing requisites; monastics sharing the Dharma; and all of us sharing this path together that leads to the end of every kind of suffering.

Reflect:

-Why is the relationship between monastics and householders called mutual dependence?

-How does the interaction between Sujata and the Buddha demonstrate this mutual dependence?

-How does an "economy of gifts" chart a middle path between the extremes of luxury and asceticism? Between the economic realities of wealth and poverty?

-What does an "economy of gifts" teach us about creating healthy, compassionate, and wise societies?

Practice:

-Using the ***Bahukāra Sutta*** as a guide, spend time reflecting on where you fit into this economy of gifts. Pay special attention to how gratitude and generosity go together.

-If you haven't done so already, explore ways that householders are able to support your temple and monastic sangha. Choose a way to participate that reflects the gratitude and joy you have in the practice.

-Reflect on ways that the lessons learned in an "economy of gifts" might influence and transform your interactions in other economic relationships, from how you make your livelihood to how you shop. Connect these reflections with practicing mindful consumption and the second precept, "to refrain from taking that which is not given." How do you also relate to the four requisites in a way that supports cultivating wisdom and compassion?

16. The Fragrance of the Dharma

Flame and smoke disappear,
while the fragrance of incense lingers.

May the fragrance of the Dharma
linger in the heart-mind.

The religious tradition of my childhood was intentionally sparse when it came to beauty. A simple wooden cross might hang on the wall behind the pulpit, and a vase of flowers might sit on the communion table. The emphasis was on listening to the sermon, and anything else was a potential distraction to be avoided. We even joked that the pews were uncomfortable so we would have no choice but to sit up straight and pay attention.

The first time I visited a Buddhist temple was a contrast, to say the least. Even though unfamiliar, I could recognize the care to express beauty and teach the Dharma through all the senses. Chief among these lessons was impermanence. Flowers are a fitting offering, beautiful to see and smell, but they wilt. Water and tea offerings evaporate. Food offerings spoil and rot. Candles burn out. Photos and paintings fade. Statues collect dust. A bell does not ring forever. You must tend the altar with attention and care. This is an image of our practice, too. If we want to cultivate wisdom and compassion, we can't neglect our practice any more than we can neglect an altar.

In many Buddhist traditions, these common offerings are also connected with our own impermanence. They evoke the four elements of fire (candles and lamps), water (water and tea), earth (fruit, flowers, and food), and air (incense). Observing the impermanence of our offerings invites us to reflect on the impermanence of our own bodies. Incense is especially prominent in offering us this reminder; we can clearly observe how a lit stick of incense is soon smoke and ash, and burners are commonly filled with the ash of past incense. Meditation may even be timed with a stick of incense, marking the minutes and teaching us that our lives are also getting shorter. We are living processes, made of the same stuff and not exempt from the change and decay we see in our offerings. So, we reflect: how can I make the most of this precious, wonderful moment? We remember and repeat: tend the heart-mind with attention and care.

But incense also carries another meaning, as a symbol of wholesome, skillful action. There are both individual and collective aspects to this. **The *Dhammapada*** compares virtue with the fragrance of flowers and incense, but virtue is supreme because "the fragrance of the good spreads upwind; / a true person's virtue spreads in every direction." We are encouraged to string together skillful actions like a garland of flowers. On a path that takes us to the end of suffering, virtue is essential, replacing harming ourselves and others with wise and compassionate care. The very poisons to our practice are those that lead us into greed, hatred, and delusion. The virtuous antidotes are generosity, kindness, and understanding.

The collective aspect arises as we support each other, creating a community of mindful compassion. In a passage from "**The Group of Threes**," the smell of rotting fish is contrasted with the smell of powdered incense – which would you rather wrap in a leaf and carry with you? Moreover, the leaf takes the fragrance of whatever is wrapped inside it. This teaching points out that we also take on the fragrance of those around us. If you don't want your practice to end up smelling like the spiritual equivalent of rotting fish, seek out people who will support the cultivation of wisdom and compassion, leading to Awakening. We tend to become like our friends, just as a leaf takes on the smell of the incense wrapped inside it, so it is important that we pay attention to the habits we create in community.

For all these reasons, offering incense can be a supportive and wonderful practice in our daily lives. In a well-known incense offering that we often recite, we begin with gratitude. Our hearts naturally open with thanks when we remember the great gift of the Dharma – beautiful all the way through, in the beginning, middle, and end. We join this gratitude with a double aspiration. First, may our practice itself become an offering that is as fragrant as the incense. Second, may we practice for the benefit of all beings. We then dedicate the merit of our practice to the wellbeing of all who have helped us on this journey, especially the Triple Gem. In this way, we remember that the fragrance of the Dharma is lovelier than even the loveliest incense, suffusing our acts of body, speech, and mind like the fragrance of incense lingering in the Buddha Hall.

Reflect:

-How has your practice been shaped and deepened by your temple's and tradition's architecture, art, altars, and rituals?

-In particular, how do incense offerings help us practice with impermanence in a grateful, kind, and insightful way?

-What does it mean for your own practice to contemplate how virtuous acts of body, speech and mind carry the fragrance of the Dharma? How do the personal and collective aspects support each other?

-Why does the incense offering connect gratitude with an aspiration to practice? How do these two relate to sharing the merit?

Practice:

-If it is not already your practice, ask for instruction on offering incense at your temple. Try to make this offering a habit. (If you have chemical sensitivities, you can also explore alternative offerings.)

-If possible, set up a small altar at your home as part of your practice. Pay attention to how the daily upkeep of your altar supports, connects to, and reflects the importance of your larger Dharma practice. If you are able to offer incense or other fragrances (such as aromatherapy), recite or chant your tradition's incense offering.

-Intentionally make room for studying and cultivating virtue as part of your practice. This may include contemplating the Five Precepts, practicing generosity, cultivating *mettā* (lovingkindness), and similar practices. Take care to also reflect on how you spend your time and with whom, surrounding yourself with people and habits that support your mutual wellbeing and the cultivation of wisdom and compassion.

17. A Path to the Present Moment

Following the sound of the bell,
like a path to the present moment,

we joyfully accept the invitation
to live deeply in the here and now.

Many years ago, a group of us were backpacking in the Mark Twain National Forest. We were three days into a four-day loop when the trail disappeared. Scouting around, we found that several trees had fallen earlier in the year, the trail had been buried by leaves and branches, and the path had been further hidden by disuse. We didn't have the supplies or time to turn around, so we decided to cut across the forest to meet up with a creek. Using our map, we found our way, safely following the creek back to the recreation area.

Paths have long been a metaphor for the spiritual life, but the image of a path is built into Buddhism, prominent from the beginning in the Fourth Noble Truth, which is the Eightfold Path. A Buddhist proverb reminds us that "the sutras are a path." The emphasis is not on mental assent, to believe "the right thing." Instead, we focus on practice, and Right View emerges out of this direct experience. The more we practice, the more deeply we understand; the more we understand, the more deeply we practice. The teachings are a path: they take us nowhere if we do not put them into action.

But the Buddha understood how easy it is for us to get lost. Our ignorance blossoms into greed, hatred, and delusion. Our minds run to the past, recalling our rage and regret for the unpleasant experiences that we hated, or our delight and desire for the pleasant things that we loved. And our minds run to the future, dreading all the fears and anxieties for unpleasant experiences that might come our way, or hoping for all the blessings and benefits we crave. The path disappears just as thoroughly as a trail buried under leaves in the woods.

The practice, then, is to come back to the present moment and compassionately understand things as they are. In **the *Bhaddekaratta Sutta***, the Buddha answered the question of what makes a day a truly auspicious one. Rather than relying on the whims of cosmic forces for good luck, he taught that the path of wisdom and compassion is something we cultivate right here, in the present. After all, even our thoughts of the past and future only exist in this moment. To understand, heal, and transform them, we must face and "clearly see" them, right now. "Knowing this, foster it — / unfaltering, unshakable," the Buddha said. "Today's the day to keenly work".

To help us along, Buddhist practice is filled with reminders, invitations to return to the present moment. The bell is perhaps the most well-known of these reminders. It is compared to the Buddha's voice, a beautiful sound that cuts through ignorance and wakes us up. As such, we may collectively pause, for example, to listen to the sound of the bell and come back to our breathing while we go about our daily activities. We can also invite the bell to sound in ways that remind us of the Buddha's teachings, such as offering three bells to remember the Triple Gem, or four bells to remember the Four Noble Truths.

With the bell, we also return to the unity of wisdom and compassion. The bell is open and hollow: it is the emptiness of a bell that allows it to sing. But a bell offers no sound unless invited, and the quality of a bell's tone reflects how we do so. The skillful bellmaster knows and understands the bell: its tone and overtones; its depth and brightness; its harmonics and resonance. We learn this by practicing and paying attention. Similarly, wisdom is insight into the empty nature of all dharmas, and compassion is the skillful means (the form) to encounter this insight in a way that realizes Awakening encompassing all beings. The Buddha described "the heart's release by love" in **the *Subha Sutta***. It's been developed so that: "above, below, across, everywhere, all around, they spread a heart full of love to the whole world—abundant, expansive, limitless, free of enmity and ill will."

This is the return we make when we follow the sound of the bell back to the present moment, joining emptiness and form, wisdom and compassion. We are not lost in the past or the future, nor are we dragged about by greed, hatred, and delusion. We cultivate the boundless heart, offering kindness and equanimity for every being – just as, when we invite a bell, the sound radiates in all directions. "Knowing this, foster it," we hear the Buddha say: "unfaltering, unshakable."

Reflect:

-Why are the teachings described as a path? What does the metaphor of a path mean to you and your practice?

-How do we work here, in the present, with our thoughts of the past and future? How is this different from running back to the past or hoping for the future?

-Why is inviting a bell such a powerful symbol and practice in Buddhism? Which of the bell's practices and meanings have most shaped your own path?

-Why does inviting a bell embody the unity of emptiness and form, wisdom and compassion?

Practice:

-If possible, ask your teacher to explain and demonstrate how to invite the different bells used at the temple. Become familiar with when, how, and why each one is used, paying attention to any special meaning or function they each have.

-If you don't already do so, invite a bell as part of your daily practice. For example, you can invite the bell: during your chanting and meditation; at set times during the day as a way to become aware of the present moment; or when you feel a strong emotion and want to pause and get in touch with your body, feelings, and thoughts. Pay attention both to the skill involved in inviting the bell and to how your energy and mood impact how you invite it.

-Incorporate a bell into your mettā practice. Invite the bell as you contemplate cultivating goodwill for yourself and all beings. Visualize your kindness and equanimity radiating in all directions, along with the sound of the bell.

18. Already Waiting

You don't need to go far
to see the entire universe.

Look! It is already waiting
inside this humble cup of tea.

Growing up in the Ozarks, I found myself at home with the beauty of a glade, the drooping petals of a coneflower, the cool relief of a cave, the meandering peace of floating down a creek, and the spectacular acrobatics of a scissor-tailed flycatcher. My family didn't travel much or very far, but I did spend a lot of time camping, hiking, backpacking, and floating. One summer day after my senior year in high school, I was hiking with a good friend at Hercules Glades Wilderness. It was a lovely day, passing through limestone glades, resting at the little falls, and climbing the fire tower. As it became clear that we were nearing a return to the trailhead, though, my friend looked disappointed. “That was … it?,” she asked.

My friend’s experience was different from mine, after all. She had traveled extensively, including spending a lot of time in national parks. “After such a long hike,” she commented, “I’m just used to a bigger pay off. Something, I don’t know, more impressive.” The mind is often like this. It craves the novel and new, the big and bright, the special and unique. It comes out in many ways: because “the grass is always greener on the other side,” we may feel pressure to “keep up with the Joneses.” If we don’t, we’re left with an aching “fear of missing out.” These turn out to be more shortcuts, not to wellbeing and liberation, but to getting lost in the past or the future, dragged about by greed, hatred, and delusion. This isn’t to say that you should not enjoy hiking at a spectacular national park. But even then, what is to keep us from wishing we were at another, even more beautiful, place?

Something like this can easily happen when it comes to our practice. We may attach to an idea that meditation will yield some fantastic results and become frustrated when we find the practice is often made up of patiently getting to know our own heart-minds, with all the boredom, restlessness, ill-will, doubt, and desire that so often rattle around in there. Maybe there’s another teacher, another technique, another book, another posture, another cushion, another *something* that will finally work. And while we need to nourish the aspiration to practice skillfully, the desire to have a great meditation session, or to be a great meditator, may even lead us away from an actual, ongoing practice. It is easy to turn aside from the present moment, with the thought: "I just need a bigger pay off. Something, I don't know, more impressive."

Like the bell, we turn to something common to remind us that, wherever we are, this moment and this place is where we practice. Drinking tea with mindfulness, we touch the wonder that is held in a simple cup. Just as the emptiness of the bell is what makes it sing, the emptiness of the cup is what allows it to hold our tea. So we begin by sitting with gratitude. We bow to the cup; we bow to the tea. We may contemplate how extraordinary it is that we are alive for this moment, and what a gift it is to have water to drink and tea to brew. Drinking the tea is then an opportunity to be in touch with all our sense bases. We hear and see the tea being poured into the cup. We pause to smell the aroma. We feel the warmth radiating from the cup to our hands. We taste the subtle flavors.

With the mind, we also contemplate how the entire universe is held in the cup of tea. We see the conditions that brought us to this moment, from the engineers and laborers who made sure we have clean water to drink to all the people who grew, harvested, prepared, packaged, shipped, and delivered the tea. We visualize the tea plants themselves, perhaps rooted on a mountainside, soaking up sun and rain. Suddenly, we find ourselves the recipients of a cosmic generosity. Where could we possibly go, what could we possibly do, that could be more spectacular than this realization?

With awareness, we pass beyond the competition for the award of most impressive moment. We can plan a trip to a national park without diminishing the joy of a walk around the block. We can be grateful for a transcendent moment of meditative insight while still appreciating the everyday importance of befriending our boredom. And we can sit down with a humble cup of tea to find that we don't always have to go anywhere at all, because the universe has already come to us.

Reflect:

-When have you noticed a frustration with the more mundane aspects of practice? Why is working with the mundane an important part of the practice?

-Why might a "desire to have a great meditation session, or to be a great meditator, ... lead us away from an actual, ongoing practice"?

-How does drinking tea with mindfulness of the body help us come back to the present moment? How might this habit help us bring mindfulness into more of our daily lives?

-What does passing "beyond the competition for the award of most impressive moment" mean to you?

Practice:

-Choose an everyday activity, such as brushing your teeth, and approach it as a mindfulness practice. Pause before starting to cultivate gratitude, and then make each part of the activity an object of attention. Try to stay grounded in your body and in that sense of gratitude.

-Similar to the practice of "what went right" (chapter five), choose an everyday activity and list all the things that made it possible. Begin with your own existence, then move through noting practical considerations, and conclude with seeing how this activity connects with the cosmic generosity that makes life possible.

-Practice tea meditation. If possible, participate in mindfully drinking tea with others at your temple.

19. This Moment Holds Enough

The spoon is my teacher:

this moment
holds enough
for this moment.

Not reaching for the next bite,
I eat with gratitude.

One of **the ten things** the Buddha said a monastic should reflect on, over and over again, was that our lives are dependent on others. As we contemplated in our reflections on mutual dependence, the existence and practice of the sangha is made possible by the community's gifts of food, medicine, robes, and shelter. Awareness of this instills a sense of immediacy, gratitude, and commitment. Each gift is precious and is treated as such. It is given to support the practice and to extend the generous sharing of the Dharma. Taking only what is needed becomes an expression of grateful and mindful use of the requisites.

From the beginning, the begging bowl has been an intentional tool for practicing and teaching this gratitude and generosity. Often called the "bowl of appropriate measure" (*ứng lượng khí*), it brings the giver, receiver, and gift together, without separation. The bowl is meant to hold enough food for the day, because this is the only day we have to practice. We get a glimpse of the opposite of this wisdom in the ***Donapaka Sutta***, where King Pasenadi eats his food "by the bucket." A bucket, it turns out, is not an appropriate measure for a human being, and the king was suffering. The Buddha offers him an alternative:

> "When [you are] always mindful,
> knowing moderation in eating,
> [your] discomfort fades,
> and [you age] slowly, taking care of [your] life."

But if it brings suffering, why is mindless eating such an easy habit to fall into? Eating today is a complicated business. Our industrial food systems have transformed agricultural, processing, and distribution practices. This has reduced scarcity in some ways, while increasing it in others. Our food often travels thousands of miles, from different continents, and may be processed and packaged many times along the way. Economic pressures and disparities create other limitations, with the greatest obstacles placed in front of our most vulnerable communities. Thousands of food deserts in the USA leave millions of people at risk. Add to this our cultural tendencies to eat quickly and heedlessly, and we can see that we are encouraged in our greed, overwhelmed by stress, surrounded by distractions, and consumed with our thoughts. We are not well supported in mindful eating. Addressing these issues is our collective work, so that everyone can have access to healthy, nutritious food.

Along the way, the Buddha invites us to take care of our lives in whatever ways we can, to bring wisdom and compassion into each moment. Eating mindfully is a good step. We need an appropriate measure, a practice that can hold our gratitude and awareness. Eating can then become an opportunity for insight and kindness, to know that we are truly sustained by the entire universe. A meal is a moment when we can know this generosity and learn to pass it along. We contemplate the empty bowl, and we take only what we need. (Especially in our society, which tends to confuse consumption with happiness, it is generally a good practice to take a little less than we think we will need.)

To bring this awareness to each bite, we can also consider the spoon as an instrument of appropriate measure. Notice when and how the mind is already leaving the present moment, reaching for what is next. You may enjoy setting the spoon down in between each bite, simply staying with what the spoon can hold. Another common piece of advice is to chew each bite 30 to 40 times before swallowing. You don't need to fill the spoon again until then. And as others have instructed us, with mindfulness you can learn to stop eating five bites before you are full. Pay attention, eating with awareness and gratitude.

We can take this practice into the rest of our lives, too. When we get lost in the past or the future, it is like using a bucket instead of a bowl. The more practiced we become in participating in the economy of gifts, the more deeply we understand that each moment really is enough. It cannot hold more than a moment. Stay with it, "taking care of [your] life," well-nourished with gratitude, kindness, and wisdom.

Reflect:

-How does mindful eating connect with our practice of mutual dependence and the economy of gifts?

-Why is "an appropriate measure" a useful support for us? Why is mindful eating an expression of "taking care of [your] life"?

-Reflect on the complicated relationship our society has with food and nutrition, especially as it relates to economic and social disparities. How does your community support (or fail to support) access to fresh and nutritious food? How does accessing this food relate to other social issues, such as transportation, employment, housing, and health care? What challenges to mindful eating are most pressing in your own life and community?

-What mindful eating practices and appropriate measures have been most helpful to you? How are they connected with transforming both ourselves and our society?

Practice:

-Connect with a local organization that is related to mindful eating. This could be a local food producer, such as Community Supported Agriculture (CSA), an organization that addresses food insecurity, an educational group that promotes nutrition, etc. Explore ways that you could support and/or participate with that organization.

-Practice mindful eating. Choose a simple food, such as a piece of fruit, and make it the object of your awareness. Pay attention to each part of the process: choosing the fruit, washing it, preparing it, eating it, and cleaning up. Eat slowly, with awareness of each sense base. Chew each bite at least 30 times before swallowing. Set aside plenty of time to savor the experience.

-If you do not do so already, recite the Five Contemplations at least once a day before filling your bowl or plate and eating.

III. Celebrations

20. An Old Friend

Entering the Buddha Hall,
a cherry blossom greets me.

I bow in gratitude to see
an old friend in the New Year.

Blooming flowers welcome the lunar new year in southeast Asia, with yellow apricot and pink cherry blossoms among them. But when it comes to celebrating Tết in Missouri, the flowers and trees are sleeping, waiting for spring. Still, there are ways to enjoy the beauty of a cherry blossom. Cuttings with many buds are carefully harvested in warmer climes and brought to the temple. Once here, they are ready to bloom after a month or so of care. Brightening the Buddha Hall, they are beautiful reminders of joy in the present moment. It's easy to smile to the flowers and enjoy their presence, a wonderful way to begin a new year.

If you help with or witness the care involved, a blooming branch also invites us to reflect on our spiritual practice. They don't bloom by accident; they are responding to care that helped provide just the right conditions. Similarly, we work together to create and care for a temple community where wisdom and compassion can blossom and thrive. You don't wait for Tết to make sure the apricot and cherry trees have the conditions they need. You care for the trees all year long – even when they are not in bloom. If we want a practice and a temple community that blossoms into kindness and insight, we don't wait. We care for our practice and community all year long. That kind of repeated, dedicated care is what makes the beauty possible.

Repetition is often a theme in Buddhist practice. For example, visitors sometimes ask if we chant the same service every week, week after week, and they are often surprised or even exasperated by the answer: yes. There are exceptions when things change, such as during the holidays or special memorials. But most services invite us to return to familiar words and practices. Our Thầy emphasizes that this is what brings what is outside, inside. That internalization transforms an experience into a habit, and a habit into a resource. It is especially important if we want to have understanding and energy at hand to transform suffering. A skillful habit empowers us to act with more and more wisdom and compassion in each moment, including the difficult ones.

The habit begins with, and is sustained by, a clear aspiration: to relieve and even find an end of suffering. This is no small thing; the clarity helps us not get lost or distracted along the way. When we practice with the precepts, for instance, we are not merely submitting to some external rule. Instead, we are bringing the precept into our awareness as a way to better understand how suffering arises and ceases, and how that suffering and its end is connected with the choices we make, personally and collectively. The quality of attention, then, is also part of the practice. The more we pay attention, the more we find opportunities to intentionally act in ways that heal and help (instead of harm) ourselves, others, and the earth. By staying close to that skillful intention, our attention is freed to find and focus on those things that best support the path. We get better and better at both noticing when we make a mistake, as well as when we do something skillful. We then get better and better at noticing when we are about to do something harmful (avoiding that action) and when we have an opportunity to do something wise and kind (choosing that action). This is Right Effort, the habit of noticing and letting go of harmful actions while noticing and strengthening skillful ones.

Buddhist practice also provides a tradition with teachers and communities to support us along the way. We do not need to recreate the proverbial wheel, especially when the Wheel of the Dharma has been so plainly laid out by the Buddha and practiced faithfully by so many through the years. When we practice with a teacher and community, we free up time and energy for the actual practice. And where adaptations need to be made, we have support and care to do so skillfully, instead of haphazardly. A community can also help us sustain our practice, especially when we are confused or overwhelmed, helping us find encouragement, celebration, motivation, instruction, and correction when we need it.

Care for the trees all year long, and you will likely have beautiful blossoms at the new year. Likewise, it is deliberate practice that makes beautiful, wholesome, insightful, liberating moments in our lives possible. The flower may bloom in a momentary burst of beauty, but it grows out of the seed, soil, sun, and rain. And when we smile to the new year flower, we also smile to all the work the tree has done to be rooted and grow, making that blossom not only possible, but real.

Reflect:

-What are some of the lessons that you have learned from flowers? How have flowers been a part of or influenced your practice?

-Celebrating the new year brings together old and new. How is this like Buddhist practice? Consider the many aspects of a healthy practice, such as:

- focus on a clear and wholesome aspiration;

- identify and practice skills that support that intention;
- cultivate Right Effort;
- connect with a tradition and community for mutual support and accountability; and
- celebrate with gratitude and joy.

-What aspects have you already been able to make into a habit? In what areas would you like to grow during this upcoming year?

-Return to the idea that: "Care for the trees all year long, and you will likely have beautiful blossoms at the new year." How does this relate to your own experience and practice?

Practice:

-If you are so inclined, incorporate caring for a plant into your practice, whether planting a garden, tending an indoor plant, or bringing cut flowers into your home. Notice how the daily practice of care connects with caring for your Buddhist practice.

-Attend your temple's lunar new year celebration. If possible, help out with any special decorations, preparations, cleaning, or other practical aspects of making a beautiful celebration possible.

-Consider again the many aspects of a healthy practice. Set aside time to reflect and identify ways that you are already practicing each aspect, as well as challenges you have faced and are facing. Make sure to pause often to cultivate gratitude and celebrate the way your practice supports you in healing and growing toward Awakening.

21. Each Moment as a Gift

Experiencing the new year as a gift,
we express gratitude with offerings
of incense, flowers, tea, and fruit.

Experiencing each moment as a gift,
we express gratitude by cultivating
wisdom, generosity, and kindness.

Gratitude and generosity have been themes throughout these reflections, and they are present here, too, at Lunar New Year. The halls teem with decorations, the tables hold special new year foods and flowers, the shrines overflow with offerings, and red envelopes change hands. There is laughter, singing, and bright clothing in the Dharma Hall, and cheerful lights, cherry blossoms, and water offerings in the Buddha Hall. Life is uncertain, and yet we are here, together, to mark a new year. The new year reminds us of this, an invitation to experience time as a gift and, in turn, practice generosity.

Generosity is closely related to kindness and goodwill, but our practice of it at the new year reminds us that it is also closely related to impermanence. All our incessant I-making, my-making, and mine-making provide our grasping an easy place to hide. But because all conditioned phenomena are impermanent, there is no question of letting go. We practice this daily when we recite **the Five Remembrances**:

> "I am liable to grow old, I am not exempt from old age. ... I am liable to get sick, I am not exempt from sickness. ... I am liable to die, I am not exempt from death. ... I must be parted and separated from all I hold dear and beloved. ... I am the owner of my deeds and heir to my deeds. Deeds are my womb, my relative, and my refuge. I shall be the heir of whatever deeds I do, whether good or bad."

Practicing generosity is another path to this skillful familiarity with impermanence, especially bringing us back to the third remembrance: "I must be parted and separated from all I hold dear and beloved." What we hold "dear and beloved" can be people, self-views, ideas, possessions – anything that stirs in us that grasping of "me" and "mine." That grasping is often subtle, difficult to recognize. But impermanence is a powerful lens through which to spot it, because grasping contains with it a rebellion against impermanence. Usually, all it takes is bringing to mind one of those “dear and beloved” things and paying attention to the reactive feelings. Often, just below the experience of something as “dear and beloved” is an experience of anxiety, fear, or even rage at the prospect of letting go.

But this is not an inevitable path. If we can pause the spiral of grasping, we can shift into gratitude. What makes this “dear and beloved”? We can move attention to those elements that support wellbeing and bring joy. “I must be parted and separated from all I hold dear and beloved.” Grasping rebels against this reality, but gratitude opens to it. In this moment, I am not separated, so I gratefully bring my mindfulness to the relationship and experience right now. Or, in this moment, I have an awareness that the beloved experience is passed, so I bring my mindfulness to the gratitude and the grief that helps transform loss into wisdom and compassion.

Generosity provides a space to cultivate this art of letting go in the course of everyday life. We can learn to recognize when and how that grasping arises, befriend it, and consciously bring our relationship with impermanence into the practice. When an inclination to generosity arises, we can also observe the grasping mind. What does it mean to call something mine? Why is this mine to give? When does something no longer belong to me? What does it mean to keep something? What does it mean to care for something? What does it mean to share with others? How do I relate to this object I call mine –

with grasping or with openness? In the new year, we get another glimpse of that "**economy of gifts**" and what it may look and feel like when gratitude and generosity replaces grasping. A teacher of mine once told me: "Hold everything in life with open hands; it hurts less when you let go." But holding everything with openness also hurts less in the holding. We can learn to take things up and put things down with freedom, understanding when it is skillful and useful to do so. Being well-practiced in letting go, we continually move from grasping to gratitude and generosity. This new year is a gift, as is each moment. With gratitude, we share in the generosity and pass it on.

Reflect:

-How does celebrating the Lunar New Year bring impermanence, gratitude, and generosity together?

-What are some of the ways that our incessant I-making, my-making, and mine-making provide grasping an easy place to hide? When have you noticed that grasping contains with it a rebellion against impermanence?

-How does working with impermanence deepen gratitude in your own life and practice?

-How has practicing generosity helped you encounter and transform your relationship with impermanence?

Practice:

-Intentionally practice generosity in preparation for and celebration of the Lunar New Year. For example, make a daily offering of fruit or flowers at your home altar; give an extra donation to your temple or teacher; support or volunteer with a local organization that is dedicated to your community; or give a special gift to a friend or loved one. As you pay attention to generosity as a changing, impermanent process, intentionally stay with, and return to, gratitude and goodwill.

-Return to the Five Remembrances. For each recollection, take note of how you are relating to impermanence. What are some of the differences you notice when you approach those recollections with grasping, in contrast with gratitude?

-Contemplate generosity as a space to cultivate letting go in everyday life. For example, you may reflect on questions such as these:

- What do I mean when I call something mine?
- When does something no longer belong to me?
- When do I relate to this object I call mine with grasping? When do I relate to it with gratitude and openness?
- How does this grasping bring about suffering? How does this gratitude and openness bring about understanding and generosity?

22. Closing and Opening

One year closes as another opens,
like the falling and rising of a breath.

May we practice so that
peace and harmony
unfold with each rising
and setting of the sun.

Though the most obvious aspect of impermanence is that everything is changing, that change often hides in plain sight, obscured by our constant grasping at permanence. At the new year, we pause to acknowledge that the moments that make up our lives are, in fact, a continual stream of change. So here we are, thinking about what the last year held and what the next year may hold. Within this reflection is the insight that each moment presents us with an opportunity to cultivate wisdom and compassion, and the shape of our lives, communities, histories, and cultures arises out of those decisions. And further: we are always practicing, we are always training the mind, whether we recognize it or not. It is happening personally and collectively, whether we recognize it or not. Together, our actions of body, speech, and mind help create the conditions that will give rise to the conditions that follow. This is karma-vipāka, actions and their ripening.

It is important that this reflection empowers, rather than obscures, the role of practice in all of this. Looking backwards, we may notice a discernible thread that brought conditions together, which may carry with it a sense of inevitability or even determinism. The Buddha addressed important misunderstandings about karma in the ***Tittha Sutta***, all of "which, when taken to their conclusion, end with inaction." As we grow in insight about karma-vipāka, we come to understand how suffering arises – and how it comes to an end. This is why the Buddha corrected those misunderstandings by including a summary of the Four Noble Truths. The opportunity that the Buddha's teachings offer to us is to intentionally, purposefully, and persistently act in ways that bring about less suffering, more wisdom and compassion, and the possibility of Awakening.

The more we practice this way, personally and collectively, the more our confidence grows. We gain more understanding and compassion for the importance of skillfully relating to conditions: our actions of body, speech, and mind. Our own temple's existence is a beautiful example of this. When I returned to this small city in 2010, Định Quang Temple was just beginning to form, and our Venerable Thầy arrived the same year. Services were held in a converted house, and my first visit was to a crowded 2011 Ullambana celebration. I was very much a visitor: warmly welcomed, but a stranger and unknown. I could not have guessed that my visit then would open to this path. It is strange to remember that my life did not yet include this community or teacher. These were all seeds, still hidden in the ground.

This brings us back to impermanence and karma-vipāka. It is common for reflections on impermanence to conjure fear and anxiety because the mind so quickly focuses on loss. A helpful practice question I ask myself is simply: are you as wise and compassionate right now as you aspire to be? Short of enlightenment, the answer is no, and impermanence is your friend. It is what makes healing from greed, hatred, and delusion possible. It is what makes growing in generosity, kindness, and wisdom possible. To walk the Noble Eightfold path is to be open to this kind of change. Grasping at self-view, relationships, possessions, ideas, or other impermanent conditions ultimately blocks that healing and growing.

Ajahn Sucitto described this stuck-ness and how the effects of our actions add up, solidifying a pattern and giving "rise to the sense of continuity" that we confuse with a permanent, unchanging self. When we grasp at identities and conditions, craving the permanent, we lose the insight of impermanence and forget the importance of the practice. **A teaching by Thanissaro Bhikkhu** has been especially helpful to me in this regard. Reflecting on the Five Aggregates, he compared our attachment to them to carrying an ever-growing bundle of bricks. We think we are doing something great, grasping self-views so devotedly, and we don't even realize they are weighing us down. But if we change our intentions toward them, we can also change their function. Instead of grasping at them to create the illusion of a permanent self, we work with them skillfully to walk "a path to the end of suffering." Those reflections were the basis of a gatha I wrote for our temple's ten-year anniversary:

How heavy are the clinging aggregates,
like bundles of bricks on the back.
But laying them down, one by one,
they become a joyful path.

As our practices deepen day by day, we come to trust that the path will continue to unfold in these kinds of beautiful ways. We may be surprised at the details, while we are unsurprised by the overall shape. Looking back, we can see how the pot was filled, drop by drop - just as the year was filled with each sunrise and sunset; just as the day was filled with each in-breath and out-breath. We remember: each moment presents us with an opportunity to cultivate wisdom and compassion, and the shape of our lives, communities, histories, and cultures arises out of those decisions. As our teacher often says, "Now is the time to practice." It is the same message he has given to me for more than twelve years. And it is still the right lesson.

Reflect:

-What are some ways that impermanence "hides in plain sight"?

-What does it mean that "we are always practicing, we are always training the mind, whether we recognize it or not"? How does this connect with the Buddha's teachings on karma-vipāka?

-How does understanding the experience of the self as a continuity, rather than a fixed identity, help us work more skillfully with impermanence?

-How do the Four Noble Truths connect impermanence, karma, and Awakening?

Practice:

-Create a reminder of the simple teaching: "Now it is time to practice." You may keep things simple, such as handwriting a note, printing the sentence, or making a reminder on your phone or calendar. Or you may enjoy using a creative process, such as painting, writing calligraphy, or creating a collage. Place your reminder where you will encounter it regularly and make a habit of responding with a simple practice, such as taking a mindful breath or making a half bow.

- Recite and contemplate the ***Tittha Sutta***, with special attention to three ways that karma can be misunderstood:

> "'Everything this individual experiences—pleasurable, painful, or neutral—is because of past deeds. ... is because of God Almighty's creation. ... has no cause or reason.' ... Those who believe [any of these three doctrines] have no enthusiasm or effort, no idea that there are things that should and should not be done. Since they don't actually find that there are things that should and should not be done, they're unmindful and careless, and can't rightly be called ascetics."

The Buddha corrects these views through summarizing the Dharma, especially the Four Noble Truths. How does Right View help us transform our understanding of karma and empower our practice?

23. Two Streams of Water

In Lumbini, on that sacred day,
the sky offered two streams of water
to bathe the Buddha-to-Be.

I hold this prayer as I hold the ladle:
May my practice bring: freedom from harm,
abundance of good, and universal liberation.

Each year, Buddhists around the world gather to celebrate Vesak, also known as the Buddha's birthday (Phật Đản). It's a time to honor the Triple Gem and commemorate the birth, enlightenment, and parinirvāna of Shakyamuni Buddha. Central to most of these celebrations is a ceremony when each of us can bathe a statue of the baby Buddha-to-Be. We take a ladle and mindfully pour perfumed water three times. The ritual calls to mind the stories of Siddhartha's birth; in some versions, the earth shakes, flowers rain down from heaven, and two streams of water (warm and cool) wash over the newborn child.

When we pour water over the baby Buddha, we are stepping into that heavenly role of devas, nagas, and dragon-kings. With them, we recognize what a gift Awakening was, is, and will be to this world. And with each ladle, we bring to mind an aspiration to practice. But more, by remembering and celebrating the Buddha-to-Be, by remembering Siddhartha Gautama as a child, we recognize the Buddha nature. When we recognize and care for the baby Buddha-to-Be, we also learn to recognize and care for our own Awakened Nature. When we travel throughout our day with this kind of intention and attention, keenly aware of the capacity for awakening within and around us, each moment is transformed.

In **the twentieth chapter of the *Lotus Sutra***, we hear the story of Never-Disparaging Bodhisattva (Sadāparibhūta). His path diverted from what was commonly expected of a monk. Instead of reading and reciting sutras, his only practice was to bow deeply to every person he met. 'I could never disparage you,' he would say. 'How could I, when each and every one of you will become a buddha?' You may think this was an easy way out, a way to avoid the challenges of a conventional monastic practice. It was, in fact, the opposite. Many of those Never-Disparaging greeted in this way became angry, rewarding respect with ridicule. 'Who does this ignorant monk think he is, presuming to assure others that they will attain enlightenment? His words are empty lies, false assurances.'

The Bodhisattva's practice went on like this for years, trading encouragement and respect for mockery and insults. In fact, this is how he received his name, as an attempt to mock him. And when the unkind words were not cruel enough, some took up sticks and stones, beating and chasing him. But Never-Disparaging did not falter. He still saw through the anger and insults to their capacity for wisdom and compassion. Even while dodging staves or outrunning stones, he would cry out, 'I still cannot disparage you, for you are a Buddha-to-Be!'

His confidence was correct. By the end of the chapter, the Buddha reveals that he himself was that Never-Disparaging Bodhisattva, having passed through countless lifetimes, perfecting wisdom and compassion, and both hearing and teaching the *Lotus Sutra*. Moreover, all those that had belittled and mocked Never-Disparaging, having passed through their own suffering born of hatred and violence, had themselves turned toward Awakening. 'What do you think?,' the Buddha asked. 'Where are they now? They are right here, with us in this very assembly.'

I remember all of this when I bathe the baby Buddha. Awakening may feel impossible. Sometimes, we doubt our own capacity for wisdom and compassion. Sometimes, we doubt others' capacity. But one of the lessons of these stories of countless lives and myriads of kalpas is a powerful encouragement for us: keep practicing; stay on the path; do not worry; do not disparage yourself or others. It is okay that this transformation may take a long time. The important thing is that it is happening, and we can support each other on the path. After all, the Buddha was, for many ages, a Buddha-to-Be. So as I bow before the baby Buddha and take up the ladle, I remember this and utter my aspirations: "May I and all beings be free from greed, hatred, and delusion. May every action we take in body, speech, and mind be suffused with wisdom and compassion. And may all beings come to an end of suffering, awaken, and be free."

Reflect:

-Return to the three basic aspirations we cultivate while bathing the baby Buddha-to-Be: letting go, cleansing, and healing all harmful actions of body, speech, and mind; cultivating skillful actions that embody wisdom and compassion; and dedicating our practice for the awakening of all beings. How do they mutually support each other and our practice?

-In what ways does the Vesak celebration honoring the baby Buddha-to-Be connect with our daily awareness and honoring of the Buddha nature in ourselves and others?

-Reflect on Never-Disparaging Bodhisattva's need to

run from people who responded to his practice by reviling or even attacking him. Why do you think so many people responded negatively to him? How does the Bodhisattva's practice of keeping a healthy distance from them, while still refusing to disparage anyone, connect with the wisdom of healthy social and emotional boundaries?

-What is the significance of the practice of Never-Disparaging Bodhisattva? When do you most need to bow respectfully to your own Buddha nature? To others' Buddha nature? How does this connect with our celebration of Vesak?

Practice:

-Participate in a ceremony for bathing the baby Buddha at your temple's Vesak celebration. (Alternatively, mindfully watch a ceremony online.)

-Practice with the three basic aspirations we recite during the bathing the Baby Buddha ceremony. Write your own versions, based on how they connect with your practice right now. Put them in a place where you can remember them throughout the day.

-Read **chapter 20 of the *Lotus Sutra*** about Never-Disparaging Bodhisattva. Set aside a day when you can put into practice recognizing and bowing (literally and/or internally) to the Buddha nature of everyone you meet. Reflect on how honoring the capacity in all beings for wisdom and compassion, leading to Awakening, impacts your day. What insights and benefits did you notice? What struggles did you experience?

24. Undeterred

The palace behind him,
and abandoned by friends,
Gotama was undeterred.

He sat beneath a Bo tree,
with legs folded and
heart-mind resolved.

Mara was heartbroken
as the Buddha awoke,
and **fragrant flowers fell**
like a gentle rain.

"**This is good enough for striving**," thought Gotama, the soon-to-be-Buddha, at the end of his very long walk. He had lived in the extremes of palace and forest; learned with and surpassed the greatest teachers;

practiced austerities with his five companions; and set off, "traveling stage by stage," through the Magadhan lands. Now, he found himself in "a delightful park, a lovely grove with a flowing river that was clean and charming, with smooth banks." A nearby village would provide alms gifts to support him on his path, completing a pursuit that had filled his lifetime. So, when he resolved to sit in that lovely grove, he had already skillfully, patiently, persistently, carefully, and lovingly nourished the seed of Awakening for a long time. His resolution for nirvāṇa was a heavy fruit, ready to pick. "I sought the unborn supreme sanctuary from the yoke, extinguishment — and I found it."

Years later, the Buddha would reflect on that resolve, the sense of being undeterred. He had spent the day meditating deep in the Great Wood. When he emerged from meditation, **Ananda and a householder named Tapussa were waiting for him** with a question. Tapussa wanted to know what it took for a mendicant's mind to be "secure in renunciation" – the art of opening up, letting go, and getting free. The multitudes' hearts are fixed on sensual pleasures, he observed, and "renunciation seems like an abyss." So it was a stark contrast when he saw mendicants whose minds were "confident, settled, and decided" and who even saw renunciation "as peaceful." It was, he said, "a dividing line."

When Ananda reported this, the Buddha replied, "That's so true!" He recalled the years when his own mind was not settled, confident, or peaceful, even though he thought that, at least in theory, "Renunciation is good! Seclusion is good!" But instead of another obstacle, this insight became the place for practice. He did not abandon the path, returning to a life of greed, hatred, and delusion. Neither did he try to coerce himself into a renunciation that wasn't settled, confident, or peaceful. Instead, he investigated: "What is the cause, what is the reason why my mind isn't secure in renunciation, and not confident, settled, and decided about it? Why don't I see it as peaceful?" Looking and listening deeply, the insight arose: "I haven't seen the drawbacks of sensual pleasures, and so I haven't cultivated that. I haven't realized the benefits of renunciation, and so I haven't developed that."

Finally knowing the cause, Gotama had a clear way of practice, described in his teachings of the Four Noble Truths. He would look and listen deeply, until he could see those drawbacks and benefits clearly. From that point, the path steadily opened and deepened. Clarity regarding sense pleasure made it possible to find and sustain deep levels of tranquility and wisdom. He then applied this same process of investigation, looking and listening deeply to understand where he was caught, and to understand the drawbacks of abandoning the path and benefits of deepening it, to each stage of meditative attainments until, finally, there was nothing left. "And so, going totally beyond the dimension of neither perception nor non-perception, I entered and remained in the cessation of perception and feeling. And, having seen with wisdom, my defilements were ended."

It was another demonstration of the Middle Way, helping us understand how Gotama was able to be so undeterred and reach the further shore. He was not dragged along by fulfilling one sense desire after another, and he was not caught between grasping fueled by self-view and nihilistic urges to escape. Instead, he was grounded and well-supported by his practice. This is why the image of the meditating Buddha remains so central to Buddhist art. So that, whenever we feel like Tapussa did that "renunciation seems like an abyss," we, too, can glimpse a path that is confident, settled, secure, and altogether peaceful. We, too, can learn to see and develop insights into the drawbacks of greed, hatred, and delusion, and the benefits of renunciation. And we, too, can practice right there, confident that this moment and this place, is "good enough for striving."

Reflect:

- The Buddha was skilled in recognizing and cultivating supportive conditions for his practice. What do you think Gotama meant when he said, "This is good enough for striving"? What does this have to do with his Awakening? What does it have to do with your practice?

-Tapussa said that "renunciation seems like an abyss". Why might it feel like that? How did the Buddha turn this obstacle into a path?

-Contemplating the Eightfold Path, how does this approach connect with cultivating Right Resolve (Intention)? How are Right Resolve and Right Effort (Diligence) mutually supportive?

-How does the Buddha's path of cultivating insight demonstrate a middle path or third way? What role does renunciation have on that path?

Practice:

-Write down, make an audio recording, or otherwise document your own spiritual journey. What have been major turning points in your spiritual life? What have you been resolved to do, and what aspirations have guided you? What people, places, experiences, and insights have shaped your life?

-Return to your reflections on your spiritual journey. When have the steps you needed to take felt more like stepping into an abyss? When have you felt more confident, settled, secure, and peaceful? Do you notice any patterns for when and why you have felt those ways?

-Contemplate an area of ongoing spiritual growth in your own life and apply the Buddha's method. For clinging and craving that has become an obstacle on your path, you can ask: what drawbacks haven't I noticed? For any aspirations you have for your ongoing growth, you can ask: what benefits am I realizing on this path? Pay attention to how the heart-mind responds to noticing these drawbacks and benefits, as well as to how this method relies on insight rather than coercion.

-Place a reminder of the Buddha's Enlightenment, such as a picture or statue, where you will see it each day. Pause and recite a simple aspiration, such as: "All beings, including me, can cultivate compassion and wisdom. May all beings, including me, practice in a way that brings us to the end of suffering."

25. Beyond Coming and Going

Everything that begins, ends.
Everything that arises, ceases.

Beyond this coming and going,
the Self-Awakened One was totally unbound.

The description of the days leading up to and following Shakyamuni Buddha's death are detailed in ***The Great Total Unbinding Discourse***. Although the Buddha had already achieved nirvāṇa at his Enlightenment, his death marked the dissolution of the aggregates and a final release from that endless wheel of suffering called saṃsāra. In the discourse, the whole process of that parinirvāṇa, a "total unbinding," is filled with the same attention and intention that we see throughout the Buddha's life and teachings. He gives great care to making sure everything is ready, especially that the sangha is prepared to sustain itself through faithful practice of his teachings.

"Be of good virtues," he reminded them. "With well-settled thoughts, / take good care of your minds." The path to the end of suffering was well trod now, right there for "whoever meditates diligently / in this teaching and training". With everything fulfilled and ready, the Buddha meditates one last time, moving through each of the jhana states, tranquil and aware, in turn: the first through the fourth; the fourth through the first; and the first through the fourth again. "Emerging from that the Buddha immediately became fully extinguished."

That total unbinding was the fulfillment of the freedom the Buddha had realized and practiced for some forty-five years. Over and again, the suttas tell us this same story. For example, one day, **Daṇḍapāṇi the Sakyan went for a walk**. But he "plunged deep into the Great Wood," so this was not exactly a casual stroll. He was looking for the Buddha, and he found him. After the formal greetings and "polite conversation" were over, he revealed that he was also looking for trouble. He leaned on his staff and asked, "What is the ascetic's doctrine?" The Buddha saw through the words and, wisely and compassionately, refused to get drawn in. "Sir, my doctrine is such that one does not conflict with anyone in this world," he replied.

If Daṇḍapāṇi had been listening, he could have heard

a great teaching, for the Buddha went on to say: "And it is such that perceptions do not underlie the brahmin who lives detached from sensual pleasures, without doubting, stripped of worry, and rid of craving for rebirth in this or that state." It was a doctrine of unbinding. But Daṇḍapāṇi didn't hear it. Instead, he "shook his head, waggled his tongue, raised his eyebrows until his brow puckered in three furrows," and left in a huff. He missed his chance to understand where his suffering came from, and how he could get free of whatever grasping made him so combative.

Later, the monastics gathered around the Buddha, looking for wisdom instead of picking a fight. The Buddha answered their questions, describing how "judgments driven by proliferating perceptions beset a person." However, if there isn't "anything worth approving, welcoming, or getting attached to in the source from which these arise, just this is the end of the underlying tendencies to desire, repulsion, views, doubt, conceit, the desire to be reborn, and ignorance." Right there is the end of violence and wars, and even the end of "accusations, divisive speech, and lies." All that is left is Awakening, an unbinding from all "unskillful qualities ... without anything left over."

Venerable Thầy often instructs us: "Untie it; untie everything!" This is what we are practicing, to untie all these ways that we are caught and learn to relate to each experience with openness and insight. At Vesak, we remember the Buddha's example of this, from birth to

Awakening to parinirvāṇa. We remember: all conditioned phenomena are impermanent, so we will eventually let go of everything. The question of our practice is: how? Will we go on and on, grasping indefinitely, caught up in "judgments driven by proliferating perceptions"? Or will we open to wisdom and compassion, finally free of the relentless "approving, welcoming, or getting attached" that drives our suffering? The Buddha found and fulfilled the latter path, and he offered it to us. As we follow him in learning to untie everything, we can hear his **last words** with deepening insight and gratitude: "Come now, mendicants, I say to you all: 'Conditions fall apart. Persist with diligence.'"

Reflect:

-What is the significance of the Buddha taking such care in preparing for his parinirvāṇa?

-How did Daṇḍapāṇi demonstrate that "judgments driven by proliferating perceptions beset a person"? How did the Buddha demonstrate "the end of the underlying tendencies to desire, repulsion, views, doubt, conceit, the desire to be reborn, and ignorance"?

-Following from this, why could the Buddha say with confidence that his "doctrine is such that one does not conflict with anyone in this world"?

-How has practicing with the Buddha's teachings

supported your own process of untying the tangled knots of grasping and suffering? How is this connected with the Buddha's last words?

Practice:

-Read and contemplate ***The Great Total Unbinding Discourse***. Take your time to do so, spreading the reflection over several readings and days. Take special note of the care the Buddha gave to how he prepared for parinirvāṇa and how this helped set a path for others.

-Chant or listen to a recording of **the *Heart Sutra***. Contemplate the teaching in light of the Buddha's own unbinding.

-Place a reminder of the Buddha's parinirvāṇa, such as a picture or statue, where you will see it each day. Cultivate gratitude for the Triple Gem and recite a teaching or aspiration, such as The Five Remembrances or the Buddha's final words: "Conditions fall apart. Persist with diligence."

26. A Radiant Aura

With a voice like a young lion,
the noble Buddha taught the Dharma,
a radiant aura surrounding him
as moonlight in the clouds.

Those colors, now reflected in a flag,
draw together a community of all
who find his discourse still
sweet and beautiful to hear.

The ***Dhammacakkappavattana Sutta*** ("Setting the Wheel of the Dharma in Motion") tells of the Buddha's sharing the Dharma with his friends, the five mendicants. This well-named sutta is a succinct summary of the Middle Way, the Four Noble Truths, and the Noble Eightfold Path. In recognition of this auspicious moment, the "galaxy shook and rocked and trembled. And an immeasurable, magnificent light appeared in the world, surpassing the glory of the gods." This luminous aura often makes an appearance in Buddhist scriptures and stories. Here, the declaration that this light surpasses even "the glory of the gods" is a reminder to listen: this is important, more glorious than even the glories of the gods. And the gods, it turned out, agreed. "And when the Buddha rolled forth the Wheel of Dhamma," the sutta explained, "the earth gods raised the cry: 'Near Varanasi, in the deer park at Isipatana, the Buddha has rolled forth the supreme Wheel of Dhamma. And that wheel cannot be rolled back by any ascetic or brahmin or god or Māra or Brahmā or by anyone in the world.'"

That phrase – that the wheel cannot be rolled back – calls to mind the fundamental confidence we find in the Buddha's teachings and practices. Sometimes, Buddhism is dismissed as being too negative, too focused on suffering. But this is simple honesty, not despair. The Buddha did describe how suffering arises with sometimes devastating clarity, including how easy it is to get caught up and trapped in our greed, hatred, and delusion. But the diagnosis was given so that we could know the correct cure: the complete end of suffering, "with nothing left over; giving it away, letting it go, releasing it, and not clinging to it." In the face of the terrible and painful realities that characterize so much of human existence, that such a teaching and practice as this noble path exists, open to all of us, is an incredibly hopeful and transformative message. This is the message that continues to gather people together, to practice, build community, and celebrate a path that helps us navigate through suffering with more and more wisdom, compassion, and care, leading to liberation.

The Buddhist flag reflects this impulse. Banners have long decorated temples and stupas, but today's Buddhist flag was first designed in 1884. While variations continue to be used by specific nations and traditions, the World Fellowship of Buddhists adopted its current version in the 1950s as a symbol that could be used and recognized by the Buddhist community around the world. The colors are meant to evoke the Buddha's aura: blue, yellow, red, white, and orange. Each color is connected with a quality of the Buddha and his Dharma, from the cultivation of compassion and the Middle Way to the realization of virtue, liberation, and wisdom. The flag's sixth column includes all five colors, symbolizing both the fullness of the Buddha's teachings and the unity of the Buddhist community around the world.

The flag is a beautiful reminder, then, of how the Buddha set that wheel of the Dharma in motion. This is also the role that the aura played in the ***Dhammacakkappavattana Sutta***. That light is mentioned just after describing how the five mendicants are "happy with what the Buddha said" and one of them, Venerable Koṇḍañña, has a breakthrough of liberating insight. When we come to the close of the sutta, the last words are not about those declarations of gods, the shaking and rocking of the galaxy, or the glorious aura. Instead, these signs all point to something both more mundane and more powerful: a transforming encounter with the Dharma. "Then the Buddha expressed this heartfelt sentiment: 'Koṇḍañña has really understood! Koṇḍañña has really understood!' And that's how Venerable Koṇḍañña came to be known as 'Koṇḍañña Who Understood'."

And so, the wheel keeps rolling. Hearing the Dharma, insight blossoms again and again, across geographies, cultures, and centuries. That the wheel has rolled even here, in this obscure corner of Missouri, is a beautiful and powerful reminder of that divine proclamation: the "wheel cannot be rolled back ... by anyone in the world.'"

Reflect:

-Why was it necessary for the Buddha to include a focus on suffering in his teachings? Why doesn't this lead to despair?

-What symbols of community, like the Buddhist flag, have you noticed at your temple? What meaning or role do symbols play in your own practice?

-Why is it significant that the final verse of the *Dhammacakkappavattana Sutta* emphasizes Venerable Koṇḍañña's insight?

-What do the phrases "setting in motion the wheel of the Dharma" and the "wheel cannot be rolled back" mean to you?

Practice:

-Recite and contemplate the *Dhammacakkappavattana Sutta*. Reflect on what it means that the Buddha set the wheel of Dharma in motion.

-Investigate your temple's lineage and history. Learn about how the Dharma arrived and transformed the people who so diligently preserved and handed it down to you.

-Choose a book to help you study either the overall or a specific time in the history of Buddhism. How does this history reflect the confidence that the "wheel [of the Dharma] cannot be rolled back"?

27. From the Roots

My life blossoms from the roots of
my mother, father, and all my ancestors:

May this path of practice transform
our suffering into healing and peace.

Our temple has adopted the tradition of honoring parents during the Vu Lan holiday by wearing a rose: red for the living and white for those who have passed away. It's a wonderful time to cultivate awareness and gratitude: for our ancestors, especially parents; for the opportunity we have to hear and practice the Dharma; and for this chance to cultivate wisdom and compassion in this life.

The Buddha taught that it is not easy to repay your parents, and Buddhist traditions have historically emphasized the importance of gratitude to them. In **the *Kataññu Suttas***, the Buddha reflected on this, saying that parents would not be repaid "even if you were to carry your mother around on one shoulder and your father on the other, and if you lived like this for a hundred years". No amount of care is sufficient, and no amount of respect: "Even if you were to establish your mother and father as supreme monarchs of this great earth, abounding in the seven treasures, you would still not have done enough to repay them." There is more to this teaching than a quick reading might suggest. To begin, caring is understood as an expression of gratitude. In this same text, **the Buddha says** that "The true person is grateful and thankful, for the virtuous only know how to be grateful and thankful." This is a wonderful insight: there is no virtue without gratitude. And when conditions support the development of virtue, compassion, and wisdom, then gratitude naturally arises.

Ideally, we experience this in our families. **The Buddha described this dynamic** as: "I will support those who supported me." Parents serve their children by helping them understand and practice goodness while meeting their physical, emotional, and social needs. Cultures accomplish this in different ways, but the goal is the same: children are given resources and skills to navigate the world so that their needs are met and they can live fulfilling lives. When this is the case, it is not difficult for children to respond by caring for their parents in return. It is a virtuous cycle, and **a cause for great happiness**: "Caring for mother and father, /

kindness to children and partners, / and unstressful work: / this is the highest blessing."

But we also know that many people do not enjoy this kind of family life. Increasingly, people are estranged from family members, including parents and children. The Buddha was also familiar with the realities of a stressful home life. He was raised by his aunt because his mother had died while he was an infant. And though we don't know the details of how this affected the young Buddha-to-Be, his father had high expectations, expecting him to be a political leader, and he went to great lengths to influence and even control Siddhartha's life. The Buddha also witnessed the difficulties and suffering in families through decades of teaching and providing spiritual care to countless people. In the ***Sangaha Sutta***, he spoke honestly about what it takes for "sustaining a favorable relationship" and that: "If there were no such means / of sustaining a favorable relationship, / neither mother nor father / would be able to obtain esteem / and veneration from their children."

Unfortunately, this absence is all too real for many people. When this is the case, what can we do? We turn to that suffering to look and listen deeply. We honestly seek help and support we need from others. We learn to stop participating in unhealthy, harmful, and abusive patterns of behavior, and we learn to establish wellbeing in ourselves and in healthy relationships with others. **The Buddha described this** as developing the "four means of sustaining a favorable relationship," four habits that nurture healthy, mutually caring relationships:

> "Giving, endearing speech,
> beneficent conduct, and impartiality
> under diverse worldly conditions,
> as is suitable to fit each case: these means
> of sustaining a favorable relationship
> are like the linchpin of a rolling chariot."

This is another path of practice that helps us relate to our suffering in a more skillful way and that helps create conditions that support compassion and wisdom. In each situation we find ourselves in, we discern the most skillful way to respond, "suitable to fit each case". The linchpin is what prevented a chariot wheel from sliding off the axle, causing it to crash. This is the role of our practice in maintaining healthy relationships. When our family joins us in developing these habits, that is a cause for great happiness.

Sometimes, though, there is no linchpin and the only path for us is to break a cycle of harm, hopefully before the wheel flies off the axle. There is pain in that, but also peace and even some happiness. This is our practice of honoring all that is beneficial that we inherit from our ancestors while healing that which leads to suffering. Returning to **the *Kataññu Suttas***, we can be grateful for this opportunity of being alive, this chance to develop wisdom and compassion, while also being honest about both the skillful and unskillful habits in our families. And it turns out that this is how we best care for and even repay our parents. The Buddha went on to say that:

> "But you have done enough, more than enough, to repay them if you encourage, settle, and ground unfaithful parents in faith, unethical parents in ethical conduct, stingy parents in generosity, or ignorant parents in wisdom."

We encourage one another by actions of body, speech, and mind. Our growing wellbeing invites others to cultivate wellbeing – because our wellbeing is bound up together. It's a hopeful and practical approach, both when our family relationships are supportive, caring, joyful, and wonderful – and when they are not. In both cases, we can resolve and practice to create conditions where loving, wise relationships are possible: our lives themselves become a beautiful blossom that honors our roots.

Reflect:

-Return to the Buddha's words: "The true person is grateful and thankful, for the virtuous only know how to be grateful and thankful." What are some of the connections between virtue and gratitude?

-Why do you think that the Buddha taught that it is difficult to repay our parents? Similarly, why did he teach that the best way to repay them is to "encourage, settle, and ground unfaithful parents in faith, unethical parents in ethical conduct, stingy parents in generosity, or ignorant parents in wisdom"?

-How did the Buddha's own life demonstrate these insights?

-In what ways are the "four means of sustaining a favorable relationship" like a "linchpin of a rolling chariot"? How does this teaching relate to honoring our parents?

Practice:

-Participate in a ceremony at your temple that honors parents, such as the Rose Ceremony at Vu Lan. (Alternatively, watch an online recording.) Cultivate mindfulness of the different ways that gratitude for parents is incorporated into the practice.

-Reflect on the "four means of sustaining a favorable relationship": generosity; mindful and kind speech; mutual care and helpfulness; and consistency. Make a list of how your family practices (or struggles to practice) these. For each wholesome habit, practice gratitude. For each challenge, cultivate an aspiration to heal and grow.

28. The Compassionate Dharma

The Hungry Ghosts reveal to us
the true nature of greed, hatred, and delusion.

But the compassionate Dharma opens
to all the path of Awakening.

Hungry ghosts (or *preta*) play an important role in Buddhist cosmology and psychology. They are often portrayed as having somewhat human shaped bodies, but with bulging bellies and elongated arms, legs, and necks. They are constantly craving what they cannot have. In many depictions, they are ravenously hungry, but their throats are so thin that they can only swallow a grain of rice. Or, as we will see in the story of Mahāmaudgalyāyana's mother, the hungry ghost's food bursts into flame, becoming ash in its mouth. Other depictions show hungry ghosts that suffer from rotting mouths or swollen goiters, but they all share in common a deep misery.

This misery is no accident, because hungry ghosts are the karmic embodiment of greed, hatred, and delusion. They are caught in their craving, unable to be satisfied but endlessly seeking satisfaction. In many stories, the root of this misery is a stinginess described by the Sanskrit word, *mātsarya*. This is a state of grasping that makes it impossible to cultivate generosity and kindness. Obsessed with possessions and unwilling to share, every person and circumstance is viewed as a threat. Loss of status, material goods, or honor are avoided at all costs, leading not only to jealousy, isolation, and hypervigilance, but also to treating others with outrageous cruelty. In one story, a generous and kind Buddha, known for helping the poor, asked a woman for alms. But she was so filled with *mātsarya* that she was convinced that, if she shared good food, the mendicant would just keep coming back. Swept away by her stinginess, she filled the bowl with excrement, hiding it under a little food on top.

It's easy to recoil from these kinds of stories, and the disgust is intentional. But these tales also invite us to reflect on how we fall into our own traps. How could the woman possibly feel justified in offering a bowl of excrement to anyone, let alone a Buddha? And yet, she did. Our own greed and hatred usually come with plenty of justifications, all those supposedly Good Reasons for acting cruelly. This is the power of delusion, after all. Reflecting on this simple story, we can see both the misunderstandings and missed opportunities. She missed her chance to help others and to support the good work of the Buddha. She failed to understand how her wellbeing was connected with the wellbeing of others. She grasped at impermanent conditions as a way to happiness, but they ultimately failed her. They became justifications to deceive and harm others, including a Buddha. And so, she acted in ways that, even if she thought were in her best interest, only caused suffering.

With such stories, terrifying and repulsive in turn, is it even possible to relate to hungry ghosts in wise and compassionate ways? Does their *mātsarya* justify treating them in like manner? Do we respond to jealousy and greed with more of the same? No; despite their misery and terror, Buddhist stories also depict hungry ghosts being treated with generosity, kindness, and wisdom, often leading to an end of their suffering. In the tale of Jāmbāla, the Buddha meets 500 hungry ghosts who suffered terribly because they couldn't drink. The Buddha responds by giving them water to quench their thirst. Their gratitude to and faith in the Buddha is so profound that, when they died, they were reborn in a divine realm. But, realizing that their relief was due to the Buddha's compassion, they travel back to earth so they could listen to the Buddha teach. Very soon, they understand the Four Noble Truths and became stream enterers.

Hungry ghosts, then, are not only powerful demonstrations of the terrible suffering that arises from our greed, hatred, and delusion, but also of the even greater effectiveness of practicing the Buddha's teachings to relieve that suffering. To put this in terms of Right Effort, the stories of hungry ghosts can teach us to more skillfully recognize the harmful choices we make and the justifications we have for making them. We can especially be on the lookout for how *mātsarya* creeps into our lives and communities, and we can then learn to let go of and heal those cruel delusions. Similarly, we can learn how to respond with generosity, kindness, and wisdom to even very difficult people and circumstances, as the Buddha did with the 500 hungry ghosts. Especially in a society increasingly experiencing isolation, distrust, and fear, this healing and growing is as important as ever.

Reflect:

-What stands out most to you in the description of hungry ghosts?

-What are some of the ways that *mātsarya* operates in our lives and communities today? How can portrayals of hungry ghosts help us cultivate insight into greed, hatred, and delusion, both personally and collectively?

-What are some ways that Buddhist practice can help us recognize and transform *mātsarya* into generosity, kindness, and wisdom?

-Return to the two stories in this reflection. How does the woman's response to the Buddha's begging contrast with the Buddha's response to the 500 hungry ghosts?

Practice:

-Return to **the *Mettā Sutta*,** the Buddha's teaching on cultivating a heart of goodwill, joy, compassion, and equanimity. Contemplate the role of *mettā* in helping us transform *mātsarya,* especially the quality of *muditā* (appreciative joy). This verse may be especially helpful in beginning your reflections:

> "Let none turn from another,
> nor look down on anyone anywhere.
> Though provoked or aggrieved,
> let them not wish pain on each other."

-Create a reminder of the protective mother from the sutta (or similar protective image). Again, you may keep things simple, such as handwriting a note, printing the verses, or making a reminder on your phone or calendar. Or you may enjoy using a creative process, such as painting, writing calligraphy, or creating a collage. Place your reminder where you will encounter it regularly and make a habit of reciting these verses:

> "Even as a mother
> would protect with her life

her child, her only child,
    so too for all creatures
unfold a boundless heart.

“With love for the whole world,
    unfold a boundless heart:
above, below, all round,
    unconstricted, without enemy or foe.”

29. This Dharma of Rescue

His mother's suffering and
Mahāmaudgalyāyana's deep sadness
were transformed by the power of the Sangha.

Receiving this Dharma of rescue,
we also make offerings, with chants and prayers,
for the benefit of seven generations past.

In the ***Ullambana Sutra***, Mahāmaudgalyāyana has had a spiritual breakthrough called the six penetrations. Filled with gratitude, his immediate wish is to find his parents and thank them for raising him. Perceiving that his mother was reborn as a hungry ghost, and filled with compassion, he goes to make a food offering to her. But every time she lifts the food to her mouth, it turns into flaming hot coals. Feeling helpless, Mahāmaudgalyāyana is left with nothing else to do but weep – and go to the Buddha. The Buddha's response is significant: you can't do this alone. The gods and spirits don't have enough power for this situation, let alone a single person, no matter how devoted a child they happen to be.

In contrast to this powerlessness, the Buddha says he will "speak a Dharma of rescue." And, just as we saw in the story of Jāmbāla, he offered a way to bring about an end to suffering, even for those in the most desperate and difficult of circumstances – even to a hungry ghost. But that insight that the Buddha shared with Mahāmaudgalyāyana – "You alone do not have enough power" – is especially worth our continued attention. In the sutra, the Buddha directs everyone to practice together; the Dharma of rescue included turning to one another in that mutual dependence that characterizes Buddhist community. Mahāmaudgalyāyana is invited to make offerings to the sangha, and the sangha is invited to dedicate their practice to his mother's liberation. It is a powerful demonstration of both the personal and collective dimensions of suffering and liberation. And soon, Maudgalyāyana's tears are dry and his mother's suffering is eased.

In the same way, the Buddha says, communities can continue to support each other and bring healing and liberation. More, the Buddha says that this healing and liberation stretches back seven generations. We have already reflected on how ancestor veneration connects with this healing. We all inherit karmic patterns, passed down across generations, and the need to transform this woundedness and suffering into healing and growing.

Our practices and communities can become places where this can happen, where karmic formations can be understood and transformed. At Ullambana, we are invited to celebrate and embody this possibility as a community, particularly during the Hungry Ghost ceremony.

During this service, we walk through a process of transformation that can also help us understand and transform our own suffering. Specifically, it invites us to reflect on how to turn towards suffering in a skillful, compassionate way. The monastics begin by gathering at the altar and paying homage to the Triple Gem. Calling especially on Quán Thế Âm and Kṣitigarbha Bodhisattvas, they then lead us in opening the gates of hell and inviting the hungry ghosts. In ceremonial terms, they combine mudras (gestures), dharanis (special protective chants), and mantras. All of this reminds us that turning toward suffering and this kind of healing work is done purposefully; we are committing ourselves to offering the energy, effort, time, and resources that it requires. This isn't a haphazard practice, but an intentional effort to apply the Buddha's teachings as a community. Opening the gates of hell could otherwise make things worse!

The gathered ghosts are then met, not with condemnation but with compassion, with practices that open their throats to receive the nectar of compassion and their minds to receive the Dharma. These needs are not in competition. Both the need to relieve their immediate suffering and their ultimate need for Awakening are included. Similarly, our immediate efforts to relieve *some* suffering are connected with our aspiration to relieve *all* suffering. By developing generosity, kindness, and wisdom in each moment, we gradually develop the Bodhi mind and create conditions where Awakening is possible, personally and collectively. Together, we practice in such a way that we can all be freed from greed, hatred, and delusion. This is also why we complete the service by taking refuge in the Buddha, Dharma, and Sangha and then dedicating the merits to the liberation of all beings.

With such a beautiful, healing, transformative path before them, it is no wonder that **the *Ullambana Sutra*** ends by noting that the Buddha's fourfold assembly "practiced it with delight." Far too often, our societies excel at producing *mātsarya*. Moving from grasping to grasping, we are caught in suffering and the karmic patterns of greed, hatred, and delusion. These are conditions that easily create hungry ghosts. Ullambana is a reminder that this is not inevitable. We can create community where all that is skillful, wholesome, and wise can thrive, and all that is unskillful, unwholesome, and harmful can heal. May we, too, practice such a path with delight!

Reflect:

-What does the description of the Buddha's teachings

as a "Dharma of rescue" mean to you? How does it relate to Mahāmaudgalyāyana's experience of being unable to help his mother?

-Why is it significant that the Buddha told Mahāmaudgalyāyana, "You alone do not have enough power"? How does this relate to the insight that our suffering and our awakening have both personal and collective dimensions?

-What are some ways that the hungry ghost ceremony can teach us to more skillfully relate to suffering, leading to healing and transformation?

-Reflect on the contrast between how the *Ullambana Sutra* begins and how it ends. Why do you think that the Buddha's community delighted in this practice? When have you noticed your own relationship with suffering shift from feeling powerless and distraught (like Mahāmaudgalyāyana experienced at the beginning of the sutra) to practicing with delight (like the assembly at the end of the sutra)? What supported that transformation?

Practice:

-Participate in a hungry ghost ceremony at your temple. (Alternatively, watch or listen to a recording online.)

-Recite and contemplate ***The Buddha Speaks the***

Ullambana Sutra.

-Place a reminder of the Buddha, Mahāmaudgalyāyana, Quán Thế Âm, and/or Kṣitigarbha, such as a picture or statue, where you will see it each day. Pause, call to mind the image of the hungry ghosts receiving compassion, and recite a simple aspiration, such as: "May all beings, without exception, know relief from suffering, receive the gift of the Dharma, and find the path of Awakening."

IV. Gratitude & Sharing Merit

30. A Single Drop

Quan Âm rides the waves of
birth and death to deliver to us
the nectar of compassion.

In the transformation of all afflictions,
we find a single drop is enough.

One of the most compelling expressions of Quan Âm (Avalokiteśvara) is found in **chapter 25 of the *Lotus Sutra***, often presented by itself as the *Universal Gateway Sutra*. It includes a long list of "myriad sorrows" to which the Bodhisattva hears and responds: "raging infernos," "turbulent tides," "baneful winds," "attacking blades," "fearsome ghosts," chains and fetters, and "hoards of marauders." Avalokiteśvara also hears the cries of those "stricken with lust or malice or ignorance," as well as those trying to have a child. Notice that these are kinds of suffering that would have been especially realistic fears for the sutra's original listeners, and that the Bodhisattva's actions transform each of those places of terrible suffering into a doorway to wisdom and compassion.

We could draw up our own lists in the same spirit, naming those anxieties that seem somehow beyond the scope of wisdom and compassion, where gateways out of suffering are most needed in our lives. Our feelings of helplessness in the face of that suffering are in stark contrast to the power of compassion. So effective is an appeal to the Bodhisattva of Compassion that its merit is not only as great as if "someone faithfully upholds the names of Bodhisattvas as numerous as sand grains in sixty two hundred million Ganges Rivers, and offered bed linens, robes, alms food and medicines to each and every one of them for a lifetime" – its merit will also last forever. The Bodhisattva's "wondrous wisdom" transforms everything it touches, and this power reminds us again of the central role compassion plays in our practice, pointing us back to the purpose of the Buddha's teachings: the end of every kind of suffering. Quan Âm is a manifestation of this compassionate nature of the Buddha and his Dharma. There is no one, no place, and no circumstance where this compassion cannot reach. This is a universal gateway, both because it is open in all places at all times, and because all may enter. Every door is thrown open, everywhere and for everyone. Compassion is the universal gateway that turns every circumstance into an opportunity to know and experience the liberation of the Dharma. These are "blessings boundless like the ocean, worthy of reverence!"

Still, it is a practice. Sometimes we struggle to find a door, so other images come to our aid. Avalokiteśvara is often portrayed holding a willow branch. He dips it into the nectar of compassion and sprinkles it on all he blesses. What does it mean to say that these single drops of water transform our suffering? When suffering overwhelms us, when it rages like a fire or crashes like a wave, we can get lost. Nothing else exists, except for our suffering. A single drop of this nectar of compassion reminds us of the wondrous reality I described at the outset of these reflections, when I was losing touch with my capacity for wisdom and kindness. Just when we think that nothing can ever change, that our suffering is forever and our practice is somehow fruitless, even the smallest glimpse of compassion can wake us up. My desperation and doubt were no match for that single drop, and I remembered "that there was more than the suffering. Compassion was possible, even in the worst circumstances. I could receive this precious gift and offer it to both myself and others."

The practice of the single drop also brings to mind the well-known teaching **in the *Dhammapada***:

> "Think not lightly of goodness,
>   that it won't come back to you.
> The pot is filled with water falling drop by drop;
>   the sage is filled with goodness piled up bit by bit."

We can reflect on each moment as a single drop, an invitation to let compassion suffuse the present. Each moment is enough simply because it is here, in the present, where we are alive. This isn't to say that the past and future are not important. Looking back, the past helps us understand how true it is that "the pot is filled with water falling drop by drop," and that our actions of body, speech, and mind determine whether that pot is filled with greed, hatred, and delusion – or generosity, goodwill, and wisdom. Insight into this process helps us to look forward and resolve to act in ways that pile up goodness in the future. But the actual living takes place right here: moment by moment, drop by drop. Compassion is our companion as we ride the waves of birth and death, supporting us until we, too, reach the shore of awakening.

Reflect:

-Why is Quan Âm such an appropriate manifestation of the Buddha and his Dharma?

-What would be on a list of anxieties and fears for our own times? What suffering feels like it is somehow beyond the scope of wisdom and compassion today?

-How does the conception of a "universal gateway" of compassion transform the ocean of suffering into the boundless ocean of merit?

-How does the image of a single drop make this bodhisattva path a practice?

Practice:

-Return to the compassion journal you began at the beginning of these reflections. Rereading your entries, contemplate how you have grown in awareness of both compassion and its transformative power.

-The *Dhammapada* teaches that "piling up goodness is joyful." Make a list of how goodness has piled up in your own life, then reflect on the connections between compassion and joy. How has practicing compassion increased your capacity for joy? How has practicing joy increased your capacity for compassion?

- Place a reminder of Quan Âm Bodhisattva, such as a picture or statue, where you will see it each day. Pause and recite a simple aspiration, such as: "May all beings know today the compassion that transforms the poison of greed, hatred, and delusion into the nectar of generosity, kindness, and wisdom."

31. Sharing the Merit

We bow with gratitude to the Triple Gem.
On this anniversary of our temple's construction,
we especially dedicate the merit of this offering
to all who have supported our temple community
and all who benefit from receiving the Dharma here.

May what is useful support us in deepening our practice.
May what is incomplete or inaccurate
be corrected and not become an obstacle.
And may all beings be free from suffering.
Nam Mô A Di Đà Phật

Dedicating the merit may sometimes be viewed as a formality, almost an afterthought, as we come to the end of a service, Dharma class, or activity together. And over the years, I've noticed a common temptation to divide up the practice into varying degrees of importance.

Something like meditation or sutra study is viewed as the "real practice," while chanting is just "preparing the mind." Similarly, sharing the merit, may be reduced to an announcement that we are finished with whatever we've been doing. It may even be a good moment to sneak in a side conversation or start thinking about whatever comes next in the day. But this is not the case; sharing the merit is vitally connected to our practice of cultivating wisdom and compassion.

When we dedicate the merit, we are joining a stream of generosity throughout space and time. We can only share merit with others because others have shared merit with us. So before sharing the merit, we pause and acknowledge this. Our merit is well-supported by those who practiced the Dharma before us, stretching back to the moment when Shakyamuni Buddha set the wheel of the Dharma in motion. As one Pali chant reminds us: what a wonderful gift that the Buddha "still had compassion for later generations" by teaching the Dharma! And we cultivate this same gratitude when we remember our lineage. Our Thầy is part of the 43rd generation of the Lâm Tế (Linji) lineage of Vietnamese Thiền (Zen). That's 43 generations of practice, sharing the merit, and having compassion on later generations - including us!

This means that the continuation of the Buddha's compassionate generosity is also an embodiment of the bodhisattva path. Sharing the merit arises out of that insight that our wellbeing and awakening is connected. It is no accident that the words we often use to share the merit – such as “may all beings be happy!” – are the same words we often use to practice lovingkindness (mettā) meditation. Looking deeply, we understand that the boundless heart described in **the *Mettā Sutta*** is the heart of a bodhisattva, dedicated to the wellbeing and Awakening of all. When we share the merit, we are recognizing the blossoming of that wisdom and compassion in our own hearts; otherwise, what would there be to share? Through our practice, personally and collectively, we are cultivating both this aspiration and the skills to make it real. As in our reflections on the Medicine Buddha, we wish and then live in a way that “all beings have everything they need to enjoy wellbeing and walk the path of generosity, kindness, and wisdom.”

This virtuous cycle, where our growing wellbeing invites others to cultivate wellbeing, and vice versa, also helps us let go of all comparisons and competition. I have received and I have shared; there is ultimately no division between those acts or between those who give and those who receive. So, we can offer freely: “May what is useful support us in deepening our practice.” And we can let go freely: “May what is incomplete or inaccurate be corrected and not become an obstacle.” Because we understand more fully the depth of wisdom and compassion of the bodhisattva way: “may all beings be free from suffering.”

This brings us back to the twin images of the ocean of suffering and the ocean of merit. Since Right View emerges out of practice, and our deepening practice emerges out of Right View, we remember that we are necessarily and continually letting go of unskillful actions of body, speech, and mind, making room for wisdom and compassion to thrive. Sharing the merit is part of this practice, personally and collectively. We are no longer swallowed by the ocean of suffering - because the ocean of merit is more than sufficient to help us realize where misunderstanding and grasping lies. Letting go again and again, we can bring our attention to what is skillful and cultivate that. Here we find the blossoming of patience and wisdom, adding our merits to this ocean that overwhelms us, not with suffering, but with joy.

Reflect:

-What does the contemplation that we can only share the merit with others because others have shared the merit with us mean to you?

-How do these insights connect with practicing generosity, honoring ancestors, and venerating our teachers and temple lineage?

-What are some ways you have noticed that lovingkindness (mettā) meditation and the bodhisattva vow mutually support each other?

-How does the practice of dedicating the merit connect with the image of the boundless ocean of merit?

Practice:

-Dedicating merit is closely related to developing Right Resolve (also translated as Thought, Intention, or Aspiration). When we share the merit, we are clarifying our resolve, cultivating skillful aspirations, and directing our path. Contemplate the formulas for sharing the merit that are commonly used at your temple. How do those aspirations help steer your practice toward Right Resolve?

-Make a list of common ways that merit is dedicated in your tradition. (You may also appreciate asking your teacher to describe these practices.) Contemplate both how you can participate in sharing the merit at your temple and how you have benefited from the merit of others who practiced in this way.

-If you do not already do so, make a habit of dedicating the merit in your daily practice. Call to mind people who have given you support and care: teachers, friends, ancestors, parents, caregivers, and other benefactors. Allow your heart-mind to expand with gratitude for them, locating your own life as part of a living stream of skillful actions. Cultivate insight for the benefits you have received from others and joy for the opportunity to benefit others in turn. Resolve to continue to diligently practice for the benefit of all beings.

Notes

5 "The Universal Way Of Avalokitesvara Bodhisattva (Chapter 25 of Lotus Sutra)," translated by Brian Chung, is available online at: **https://archive.org/details/lotus25/page/n5/mode/2up** .

11 "The Sutra on the Original Vows and the Attainment of Merits of Kṣitigarbha Bodhisattva" is available online at: **https://www.buddhanet.net/pdf_file/Ksitigarbha.pdf** .

15 The the *Śūraṅgama Sūtra* is available online at: **https://www.buddhanet.net/pdf_file/surangama.pdf** .

16 The *Kāraṇḍavyūha Sutra* is available online at: **https://read.84000.co/translation/toh116.html** .

21 An English translation of volume one of the *Mani Kambum* is available from *Apple Books* at: **https://books.apple.com/ca/book/mani-kabum-volume-1/id897244397** .

28 "The Vows of Bodhisattva Samantabhadra Sutra" is available online at: **https://www.buddhanet.net/pdf_file/samantabhadra.pdf**.

29 Samantabhadra's arrival is described in chapter 28 of the *Lotus Sutra,* "The Encouragement Of The Bodhisattva Universal Worthy," available online at: **https://www.cttbusa.org/lotus/lotus28.asp.html**.

34 This story is found in chapter nine of the *Vimalakīrti Nirdesa Sutra,* translated by Robert A. F. Thurman, available online at: **https://www2.kenyon.edu/Depts/Religion/Fac/Adler/Reln260/Vimalakīrti.htm** .

40 These vows can be found in the *Sutra of the Medicine Buddha*, available online at: **https://www.buddhanet.net/pdf_file/medbudsutra.pdf**.

46 This description is found in the *Śūraṅgama Sūtra,* IV. "Self-Enlightenment: How to Untie the Six Knots, Meditation on the organ of hearing," available online at: **https://www.buddhanet.net/pdf_file/surangama.pdf**.

47 Venerable Thích Thiên Ân's description of the Pure Land is found in "Self-Power and Other-Power," available online at: **https://www.urbandharma.org/ibmc/ibmc2/zpzp.html** .

52 The *Mahāparinibbāna Sutta* is available online at: **https://suttacentral.net/dn16/en/sujato** .

52 The *Assu Sutta* is available online at: **https://suttacentral.net/sn15.3/en/sujato** .

52 This passage is from *the Tiṁsamatta Sutta*, available online at: **https://suttacentral.net/sn15.13/en/sujato** .

53 This saying is also recorded in the *Mahāparinibbāna Sutta.*

54 The Buddha's description is found in the *Accharāsaṅghātavagga*, available online at: **https://suttacentral.net/an1.51-60/en/sujato** .

58 This passage is found in chapter 24 of the *Dhammapada,* available online at: **https://suttacentral.net/dhp334-359/en/sujato** .

59 The *Mettā Sutta* is available online at: **https://suttacentral.net/kp9/en/sujato** .

59 Ṭhānissaro Bhikkhu makes this point in "Mettā Means Goodwill," available online at: **https://www.dhammatalks.org/books/BeyondAllDirections/Section0007.html** .

72 Chapter 21 of the *Lalitavistara Sutra* is available online at: **https://read.84000.co/translation/toh95.html** . The Thai version of this story refers to Phra Mae Thorani, Mother Earth.

73 The *Pabbatūpama Sutta* is available online at: **https://suttacentral.net/sn3.25/en/sujato** .

77 This story is found in the *Vāhana Sutta*, available online at: **https://suttacentral.net/an10.81/en/sujato** .

79 The *Lokavipatti Sutta* is available online at: **https://suttacentral.net/an8.6/en/sujato** .

79 Venerable Udāyin's praise can be found in the *Udāyit Theragāthā*, available online at: **https://suttacentral.net/thag15.2/en/sujato** .

89 The Buddha described this upbringing in the *Sukhumāla Sutta,* available online at: **https://suttacentral.net/an3.39/en/bodhi** .

90 The Buddha described these austerities in the *Mahāsaccaka Sutta*, available online at: **https://suttacentral.net/mn36/en/sujato** .

91 "The Economy of Gifts", by Thanissaro Bhikkhu. *Access to Insight* (BCBS Edition), 5 June 2010, **https://www.accesstoinsight.org/lib/authors/thanissaro/economy.html** .

91 The *Bahukāra Sutta* is available online at: **https://suttacentral.net/iti107/en/sujato** .

97 This comparison is found in the "Pupphavagga" chapter of *The Dhammapada*, available online at: **https://suttacentral.net/dhp44-59/en/sujato** .

97 "Itivuttaka: The Group of Threes" (Iti 50-99), translated from the Pali by Thanissaro Bhikkhu. *Access to Insight* (BCBS Edition), 30 November 2013, **https://www.accesstoinsight.org/tipitaka/kn/iti/iti.3.050-099.than.html** .

102 The *Bhaddekaratta Sutta* is available online at : **https://suttacentral.net/mn131/en/sujato** .

104 The *Subha Sutta* is available online at: **https://suttacentral.net/mn99/en/sujato** .

113 These ten recollections are found in the *Pabbajitaabhiṇha Sutta*, available online at: **https://suttacentral.net/an10.48/en/sujato** .

114 The *Doṇapāka Sutta* is available online at: **https://suttacentral.net/sn3.13/en/sujato** .

128 The five remembrances are found in the *Abhiṇhapaccavekkhitabbaṭhāna Sutta*, available online at: **https://suttacentral.net/an5.57/en/sujato** .

131 "The Economy of Gifts", by Thanissaro Bhikkhu. *Access to Insight* (BCBS Edition), 5 June 2010, **https://www.accesstoinsight.org/lib/authors/thanissaro/economy.html** .

134 The *Titthāyatana Sutta* is available online at: **https://suttacentral.net/an3.61/en/sujato** .

135 Ajahn Sucitto, *Kamma and the End of Kamma* (2nd Edition), available for download at: **https://forestsangha.org/teachings/books/kamma-and-the-end-of-kamma-2nd-edition?language=English** .

136 "Five Piles of Bricks: The Khandhas as Burden & Path", by Thanissaro Bhikkhu. *Access to Insight* (BCBS Edition), 5 June 2010, **https://www.accesstoinsight.org/lib/authors/thanissaro/khandha.html** .

140 Chapter 20 of *The Lotus Sutra,* "Never-Slighting Bodhisattva," is available online at: **https://cttbusa.org/lotus/lotus20.asp** .

145 Mara's response to the Buddha's awakening is described in Chapter 21 of the *Lalitavistara,* "Conquering Māra," available online at: **https://read.84000.co/translation/toh95.html#UT22084-046-001-chapter-21** .

145 The description of fragrant flowers and other offerings are described in chapter Chapter 20 of the *Lalitavistara,* "The Displays at the Seat of Awakening," available online at: **https://read.84000.co/translation/toh95.html#UT22084-046-001-chapter-20** .

145 The Buddha's recollection is found in the *Pāsarāsi Sutta,* available online at: **https://suttacentral.net/mn26/en/sujato** .

146 The *Tapussa Sutta* is available online at: **https://suttacentral.net/an9.41/en/sujato** .

151 The *Mahā Parinibbāna Sutta* (*The Great Total Unbinding Discourse*), is available online at: **https://www.dhammatalks.org/suttas/DN/DN16.html** .

152 The story of Daṇḍapāṇi the Sakyan is from the *Madhupiṇḍika Sutta*, available online at: **https://suttacentral.net/mn18/en/sujato** .

154 "The Buddha's last words" are found in chapter 35 of the

Mahāparinibbāna Sutta, available online as above or at: **https://suttacentral.net/dn16/en/sujato** .

157 The *Dhammacakkappavattana Sutta* is available online at: **https://suttacentral.net/sn56.11/en/sujato** .

164 The *Kataññu Suttas* are available online at: **https://suttacentral.net/an2.33/en/sujato** .

164 The Buddha's description is found in section 13, "Covering the Six Directions," of the *Siṅgāla Sutta*, available online at: **https://suttacentral.net/dn31/en/sujato** .

164 The causes of great happiness are described in the *Maṅgala Sutta*, available online at: **https://suttacentral.net/kp5/en/sujato** .

165 The *Saṅgaha Sutta* is available online at: **https://suttacentral.net/an4.32/en/bodhi** .

169 Several "Stories of Ghosts" (Peta Vatthu) are available online at: **https://suttafriends.org/peta-vatthu/** . For further study, ***Hungry Ghosts* by Andy Rotman** (Wisdom Publications, 2021) is currently the best English language resource.

175 *The Buddha Speaks the Ullambana Sutra* is available online at: **https://www.cttbusa.org/ullambana/ullambana.asp.html** .

177 The service is based on the "Dharani Sutra for Saving the Burning-Mouth Hungry Ghosts" (*Pretamukhāgnivālāyaśarakāra-dhāraṇī*) and the "Ambrosia Sutra."

183 "The Universal Way Of Avalokitesvara Bodhisattva (Chapter 25 of Lotus Sutra)," translated by Brian Chung, is available online at: **https://archive.org/details/lotus25/page/n5/mode/2up** .

185 Chapter 9 of the *Dhammapada* is available online at: **https://suttacentral.net/dhp116-128/en/sujato** .

190 The chant is found in the "Morning Chanting" of Amaravati Monastery, available as a pdf download at: **https://cdn.amaravati.org/wp-**

content/uploads/2014/09/30/Chanting-Book-Vol-1-Web.pdf. It proclaims:

Sādhu no bhante bhagavā sucira-parinibbutopi

(It is well for us that the Blessed One, having attained liberation,)

Pacchimā-janatānukampa-mānasā

(Still had compassion for later generations.)

Photos

"Our True Heritage" – "chỉ cần một hơi thở nhẹ / là bao phép lạ hiển bày," meaning, "just a gentle breath / and you can see miracles surround you."

113 A meal is ready to be shared in the Dharma Hall.

121 Close-up of a spring blossom in the Buddha Hall.

127 A table with offerings welcoming the New Year at the entrance of the Dharma Hall.

133 Lights illuminate the offerings of bottled water and the main altar in the Buddha Hall in preparation for a New Year tea ceremony.

139 Close-up of the basin and the baby Buddha-to-Be for the Vesak celebration.

145 A marble lion in the courtyard, evoking both the Siddartha Gotama (the lion of the Shakya clan) and the protective presence of the Bodhisattvas.

151 Shakyamuni Buddha at his parinirvāṇa.

157 A Buddhist flag flies in the wind along the drive.

163 Offerings fill the Ancestor's Shrine.

169 The shrine for Tieu Dien Dai Si (Burning Face) is prepared with offerings for the Hungry Ghost ceremony.

175 Monastics lead the Hungry Ghost ceremony.

183 A close-up of the vial of the nectar of compassion held by Quán Thế Âm.

189 A group photo from a Lunar New Year celebration, courtesy of Master Thầy.

All other photos by David Ketchum.

www.ingramcontent.com/pod-product-compliance
Lightning Source LLC
LaVergne TN
LVHW010654110826
845149LV00014B/3085